Biographies

SEYMOUR SIMON is a science teacher and writer, with a number of children's books to his credit. A native New Yorker, he graduated from the Bronx High School of Science and City College of New York. He has taught science at different levels. He has also acted as science consultant and reviewer for various scholastic and children's magazines and has written articles on a wide range of scientific subjects. Mr. Simon now lives with his wife, Joyce, and sons, Robert and Michael, in Great Neck, Long Island.

JOHN POLGREEN has illustrated many science books including several for the Random House Look-It-Up series. He is an active member of the Association of Lunar and Planetary Observers and of the American Association of Variable Star Observers. In collaboration with his wife, Cathleen, who is also an enthusiastic amateur astronomer, he wrote and illustrated *The Earth in Space*. The Polgreens live in Dobbs Ferry, New York, and can often be seen checking cloud formations from their 19-foot open motorboat on the Hudson River.

Cover photograph: Two kinds of cumulus clouds, fractocumulus and stratocumulus, over the Santa Fe Trail.

Weather and Climate

Weather and Climate

by **Seymour Simon**
illustrated by John Polgreen

RANDOM HOUSE SCIENCE LIBRARY
RANDOM HOUSE · NEW YORK

We should like to thank Milton J. Fayne, Supervising Forecaster, Weather Bureau, Rockefeller Plaza, ESSA, for his invaluable assistance in making available various research materials and explaining in detail the workings of the U.S. Weather Bureau.

The photographs in this book are reproduced through the courtesy of: American Red Cross: 30; American Red Cross, Miami Daily News Photo: 76-77; American Red Cross, Topeka Capital-Journal Photo: 80; Polly Berrien Berends: vi (top); ESSA Photo: 7, 42, 64, 66, 70, 79, 82, 85, 86-87, 88-89, 112-113 (top), 112 (bottom), 113 (bottom), 114, 118; ESSA Photo and American Forest Products Industries: 94 (bottom); Fritz Henle, from Monkmeyer: 93 (bottom); NASA: 4-5, 100, 102, 111, 124-125; New York Times: 17; Walter D. Osborne: 94 (top); John Polgreen: vi (bottom), 33, 56, 69; Puerto Rico Information Service: 18 (top), 92; State of Alaska, Division of Tourism and Economic Development: 18 (bottom); United Nations: 93 (top), 97 (bottom); U.S. Coast Guard Photograph: 90, 96 (bottom); USDA Photo: 14; U.S. Department of Commerce, Weather Bureau: 52-53, 58, 59, 60, 61, 62, 63, 120-124; U.S. Forest Service: 95, 96-97 (top).
Cover: Bob Leasure

Contents

1 Our Changing Weather

"Whether it's cold,
Or whether it's hot,
We will have weather,
Whether or not."

There are two things about weather of which we can be sure: we're going to have it, and it's going to change. Perhaps there is one more thing that can be added: we're always interested in the weather.

Almost the first thing most people do when they get up in the morning is check the weather. Some tune in to hear the weather forecasts on the local TV or radio stations. Others glance out the window and look at the sky. Many people do both—and then take along their umbrellas anyway.

Weather influences so much of what we do and how we do it. Should we go on a picnic today, wear a heavy overcoat, put on snow tires or chains? Is it a good day to go swimming, go ice-skating, play baseball, build a snowman, water the grass? It all depends on the weather.

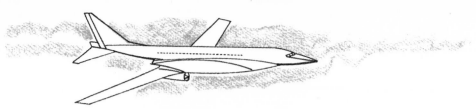

Weather even influences the way we feel. When it's a sunny spring day, with blue skies and gentle breezes, then it's just great to be out and around. But when it's one of those cold, gray, drizzly winter days, it's so much nicer to pull the covers up and stay in bed.

For some people, weather forecasts are of vital importance. Airline pilots and ship captains must know the forecast to plan their routes. Bad weather may force a pilot to land at an airport hundreds of miles away from his scheduled destination. And while large ocean-going ships can take rough weather, they too must avoid hurricanes and other violent storms.

Farmers are very concerned about the weather. Not enough rain, a sudden chill, a windstorm—these can all spell disaster. To a farmer, the weather forecast is like the stock market is to a businessman.

Many other people rely upon weather forecasts. Mountain climbers, skiers, ballplayers, snowplow drivers, cowboys, forest rangers, lumbermen, all need to know what the weather will be. So does a housewife hanging out her wash to dry, a schoolchild wondering whether to wear a raincoat, a house painter, a photographer, even a dog walker. Almost everyone wonders about the weather.

People are interested not only in day-to-day weather changes, but in the average weather and the unusual weather of a region. We call this kind of long-term weather **climate.**

Climates change with time, but not dramatically, day to day, as weather does. Over a man's lifetime,

2

climate changes very slowly. It is only by comparing weather facts over a long period of time that we can notice the change.

Most of what we know about climate and weather we have learned in the past 50 years, much in the past 15 years. Yet advances in the science of weather are coming so quickly that we can only guess at what the future holds. Whatever happens, we still will have weather, whether or not.

2 Living in the Air Ocean

We live inside the earth as well as upon it. For our planet earth is made up not only of soil, rocks, and water, but also of the gases of the **atmosphere**—nitrogen, oxygen, water vapor, carbon dioxide, argon and traces of others. We live at the bottom of the atmosphere—an enormous ocean of air. Our

4

weather takes place in this air ocean, so to understand weather we have to know something about air.

The upper part of the atmosphere reaches thousands of miles above the solid surface of the earth. Nobody knows its exact height. No sharp boundary line separates the earth's atmosphere from outer space. At that great height, gases become rarer and rarer until we can no longer detect them. Up there, the sun, moon, planets, and stars shine brightly against the blackness of space.

Our atmosphere, seen from Gemini 7, *appeared as a rim on the horizon. The sun has set but it can still be seen because its rays bend as they pass through the air.*

5

Most of the weather we see or feel or hear occurs in the lowest layer of the air ocean, the **troposphere.** (*Tropo* comes from a Greek word meaning change.) Even the highest mountain peaks on the earth are surrounded by the air of the troposphere. Varying in height from about five miles at the poles to about ten miles at the equator, the troposphere contains about three fourths of the total weight of the atmosphere.

Air seems to be the lightest of substances. But the total weight of the atmosphere is tremendous— about 5½ trillion tons. The lower you go in the atmosphere, the more closely packed are the particles of air.

At sea level, a one-inch-square column of air stretching to the top of the atmosphere presses with a weight of 14.7 pounds. In the dense air of the lower troposphere, many thousands of pounds of air squeeze against your body. Yet you have no trouble living with the air pressure at the bottom of the atmosphere anymore than a fish has with the water pressure at the bottom of the ocean. Air pressure inside your body equalizes air pressure outside your body and allows you to withstand the great weight of air.

In fact, you cannot live in regions of much lower air pressure. Airplanes that carry passengers above 10,000 feet must have pressurized air cabins. At 18,000 feet, air pressure falls to only half of what it is at sea level. You would find it difficult to breathe at high altitudes. Your lungs would seem to be bursting.

But you don't need to leave the ground to experi-

6

ence the ever-changing weather. You can feel the air when it is warm or cold, breezy or calm, wet or dry. You can see the white cotton puffs of cumulus clouds, the towering black mushroom of the thunderstorm clouds, the jagged streak of a lightning flash, the gently falling flakes of snow. You can hear the weather too: the rumble of distant thunder, the clatter of hail upon a car's roof, the rustle of the wind through the trees.

The air of the troposphere is constantly in motion.

Hailstorm over Colorado, photographed during a study of thunderstorms. The hail is falling from a cumulonimbus cloud.

7

troposphere

Great wind currents travel over the earth because of the differences in temperature at the surface. Through the constant movement of the air of the troposphere, the temperature differences between cold and warm regions are not as great as they might be.

The greater the altitude in the troposphere, the colder it gets. Air temperature drops about 3.5 degrees Fahrenheit for every 1,000 feet of altitude. This rapid temperature drop ends at the top of the troposphere in a zone called the **tropopause.**

The altitude of the tropopause changes from day to day and from season to season. At the tropopause, air temperature drops only slowly or may even rise. At this height, temperature averages about 50 degrees below zero over the continental United States, and about 100 degrees below zero at the equator. At the equator, the tropopause reaches its greatest altitude.

Above the tropopause lies the second great layer of the air ocean, called the **stratosphere.** A bit less than one fourth of the total weight of the atmosphere is contained in the stratosphere. The stratosphere

8

stratosphere

tropopause

troposphere

has little water and almost no clouds, but it does contain, at a height of about 18 miles above the ground, a thin layer of a gas called ozone.

Ozone is a special form of oxygen. The molecules of ordinary oxygen are made up of two atoms each. Some of the invisible ultraviolet waves in sunlight make oxygen atoms rearrange themselves. They form ozone molecules, which contain three oxygen atoms each.

The ozone layer is very important—it makes it possible for man to live on earth. By soaking up the harmful ultraviolet light, the ozone layer shields the surface of our planet and protects its living things. The ozone layer is also responsible for an increase in air temperature within the stratosphere. Ozone is warmed by the ultraviolet rays of the sun. It passes its heat on to the surrounding gases.

9

The gases of the ionosphere are under a terrific bombardment—light rays, x-rays and radio waves from the sun, as well as penetrating cosmic rays from space. This powerful stream of radiation is able to break apart some of the atoms in the upper atmosphere.

An atom contains protons and electrons, two kinds of electrical particles, which have opposite kinds of electrical charge. In a normal, undisturbed atom, the two kinds of charge balance out. But strong radiation can rip electrons off an atom, leaving the rest of the atom with an electric charge. The electrified atom is called an **ion.**

The mixture of ions and electrons in the upper atmosphere gathers in layers that form the **ionosphere.** It lies above the stratosphere. The entire ionosphere, which extends outward for hundreds of miles, contains only a thousandth of a percent of the weight of the atmosphere.

The ionosphere bends and reflects radio waves used in long-distance broadcasting. A long radio wave reaching the ionosphere is bent back toward the earth, from which it is reflected upward again. In this bouncing fashion, it may travel for thousands of miles around the earth. Shorter waves, such as those used in TV broadcasting, are not bent back to the earth. They pass right through the ionosphere. This helps explain the limited range of TV broadcasting stations.

The charged layers of the ionosphere change in size frequently. They increase in thickness in sunlight and are strongest at the end of the day. During the night, the layers shrink in size. The changing layers of the ionosphere produce changes in radio reception during the day and at night.

Sometimes electromagnetic storms in the ionosphere disrupt radio communication and produce brilliant displays of the northern and southern lights (auroras). The storms seem to be the result of streams of energy sent out by the sun. The streams of energy appear to be related to disturbances on the sun called sunspots.

The **aurora borealis,** or northern lights, appears at heights of about 60 miles to about 200 miles above the surface. Individual rays may go as high as 600 miles. Auroras take many forms—folded curtains of light, arcs reaching from horizon to horizon, rays

ionosphere

stratosphere

tropopause

troposphere

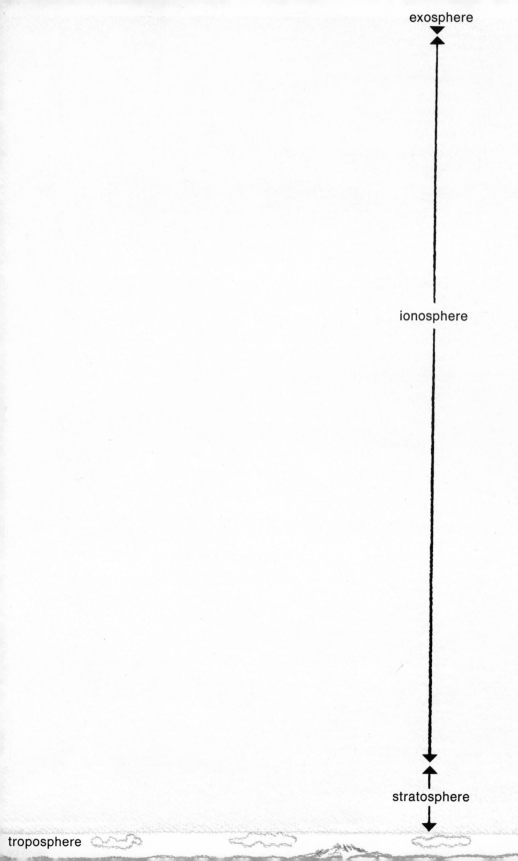

shooting upward, patches of clouds that change in brightness, and many others. Their colors range from pale white to yellow-green, red, violet, and yellow. The northern lights are visible during many nights of the year across lower Canada and the northern United States. Sometimes they can even be seen from as far south as Mexico.

Beyond the ionosphere, at heights of 350 to 500 miles, lies the earth's outermost layer of atmosphere, the **exosphere.** Here the air is extremely thin. It is made up of hydrogen and helium. The atoms and molecules of these gases are thinned out so much that they seldom meet each other and collide. At the outer edges of the exosphere, hydrogen particles escape from the atmosphere and dart off into space. Here, too, particles from space drift into the ocean of air.

Throughout the lowest 50 miles of the atmosphere the composition of air remains fairly constant. Samples of air taken from one part of the lower atmosphere are very similar to samples taken from any other part of the lower atmosphere.

Air in the troposphere is a mixture of many gases, water vapor, and tiny solid particles such as dust, smoke, pollen, molds, and salt. About 78 percent of the permanent gases of air (dry air) is nitrogen. In the atmosphere, nitrogen is chemically not very active. But nitrogen is an important element of nitrates, an essential plant food. Animals too need nitrogen in their food.

Despite the immense amount of nitrogen in the atmosphere, not enough gets into the soil to meet

Forest fire in Willamette National Forest, Oregon, in September 1966

man's ever expanding food needs. So man continues in his efforts to find an inexpensive way to use more of the nitrogen in air as plant fertilizer.

Some nitrogen combines with hydrogen and some with oxygen during high-altitude lightning flashes.

14

These nitrogen compounds are washed into the soil by rainfall. Plants and bacteria called nitrogen fixers also increase the amount of nitrogen in the soil. Other kinds of bacteria cause decay in dead organisms, returning nitrogen to the air. Thus, there is a continuous cycle of nitrogen into and out of the air.

Oxygen, chemically very different from nitrogen, makes up nearly 21 percent of the air. Oxygen is very active. It combines readily with many substances. Oxygen is needed for all forms of burning, from a flicker of a match or the oil burner that warms a house to a raging forest fire. Fires are the visible evidence of oxygen combining rapidly with some other substance. Oxygen causes the rusting of iron and other metals. It makes the cut surface of an apple turn brown. Our bodies use oxygen to change the food we eat into the energy that we need.

With so much oxygen coming out of the air, the atmosphere's supply would soon be exhausted if there were no return flow. The story of the return flow of oxygen involves another gas, carbon dioxide. Carbon dioxide makes up only about three hundredths of one percent (.03%) of air. Yet it is an important gas. Green plants take in carbon dioxide and make food of it in a process called photosynthesis. During photosynthesis, plants release oxygen back into the atmosphere. This life-giving exchange of gases is called the oxygen-carbon dioxide cycle.

Argon makes up most of the rest of the atmosphere, about nine tenths of one percent. Other gases such as neon, krypton, xenon, and helium occur in tiny amounts. All these gases are very inactive and

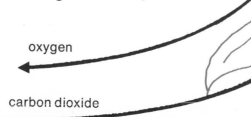

oxygen

carbon dioxide

have no known effects either on living things or on the weather.

Water vapor does. The amount of water vapor in the air varies greatly, and the differences are important to weather. Water evaporating into the air doesn't usually attract much attention, but when water is released from the air it takes the form of rain, snow, hail, sleet, fog, and clouds.

Besides water droplets and ice crystals, there are a host of other tiny solid and liquid particles in air. The most important of these are dust particles, microscopic organisms such as pollen and spores, and tiny salt particles from the oceans. When clouds or fogs form, tiny water droplets first condense on these particles.

The blue color of the sky, red sunrises and sunsets are due to the scattering of sunlight by particles. Without dust particles in the air we would still have day and night but hardly any twilight or dawn.

Dust particles are usually too small to be seen except under special conditions. When a narrow beam of sunlight slants through a dimly lit room, particles can be seen floating in air. Even a gentle breath will send them dancing in mad confusion, showing how small and light they are.

To the natural particles in the air, man has added poisonous substances of his own making. Smoke, auto fumes, oil and grease droplets, sulfur dioxide, carbon monoxide, nitrogen dioxide, all contribute to air pollution. At times, the concentration of these gases over a city becomes dangerous. This is a seri-

Thanksgiving Day 1966 smog over New York. Stagnant air mass trapped smoke and other pollutants in the air over the city for three days.

ous problem that man must face and solve. Clean air is not a luxury; it is a necessity if life is to continue.

Man constantly explores the ocean of air. With balloons and rockets he probes to the edges of space. Yet it is the weather of the lowest layers that he has known from his beginning. Clouds and rain, wind and storms, heat and cold—these will be with man so long as he lives on the earth.

17

3   The Earth's Heating System

Today is a very hot day. Today is a very cold day. Take your choice, because both statements are true. At this moment somewhere on the earth, people are going bathing to escape the heat. But at the same moment somewhere else on the earth, other people are shivering under heavy layers of clothing.

You probably know some reasons for this. The polar regions are year-round places of ice and snow, while many lands around the equator remain hot all year long. But this is only part of the answer. Seasons on the southern half of the earth are just the opposite of ours. For us, summer begins in June and winter begins in December. For the people of the Southern Hemisphere, winter begins in June and summer begins in December.

19

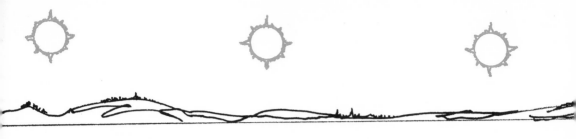

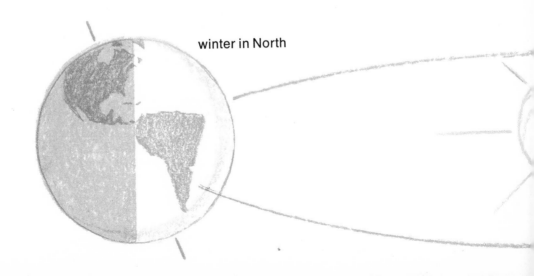

Summer in the Arctic: the sun seen at 20-minute intervals. It appears to move along the horizon without setting.

You can see that the seasonal change from winter's cold to summer's warmth is not because the earth is closer to the sun in hot weather. If that were true, our entire planet would have summer at the same time. In fact, the earth is about 3 million miles closer to the sun when winter begins in the Northern Hemisphere than when summer begins.

The seasons change because of the way the earth's axis is tilted. The earth spins, or rotates, on its axis. The axis is an imaginary line that runs through the North Pole and the South Pole. Instead of pointing straight up and down, the axis is tilted by an angle of 23½ degrees.

As the earth rotates on its axis, it also revolves around the sun in a path called an orbit. The earth takes one year to revolve once around the sun. Because the axis always slants in the same direction,

winter in North

the North Pole is tilted toward the sun during part of the year and away from the sun during another part of the year. When the North Pole is tilted toward the sun, the South Pole is tilted away.

During the time that the North Pole tilts toward the sun, the Northern Hemisphere has summer while the Southern Hemisphere has winter. We can tell the season is summer not only by the temperature but also by the length of daylight. Days are long and nights are short. For part of the year, there is no night north of the Arctic Circle. This area becomes the Land of the Midnight Sun.

Six months later when the South Pole tilts toward the sun, the Southern Hemisphere has summer while we have winter. Now the regions below the equator have the long days of summer, while in the Northern Hemisphere the days are shorter and the nights

summer in North

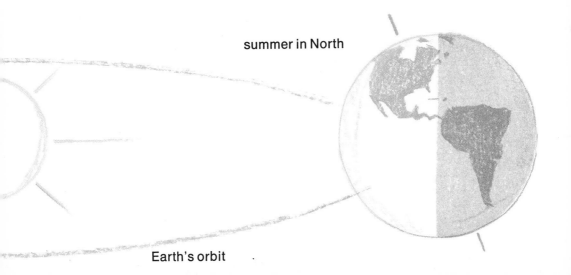

Earth's orbit

longer. North of the Arctic Circle, the sun is hidden by the horizon and the long, cold night of winter sets in.

During our summer, when the North Pole tilts toward the sun, sunlight falls more directly on the atmosphere and on the earth's surface. Direct rays concentrate the heat energy. But during our winter, the North Pole tilts away from the sun and the sun's rays come in at a slant. Slanting rays spread their energy more thinly over a wider area. Each spot receives less heat energy than in summer and the weather grows colder.

Another important reason for the temperature difference between winter and summer is the length of day. In summer the days are long and the earth has plenty of time to soak up heat energy from sunlight. The nights are short, so only a small amount is released during the hours of darkness. But in winter the ground loses more heat during the long nights than it gains during the short days.

Only about one two-billionth of the sun's energy reaches the earth. Yet the sun is so immensely hot that the earth receives all it needs from the sun. In fact, if the sun's heat were increased by a third, all life on our planet would be destroyed. On the other hand, a drop of about ten percent would coat the earth in a layer of ice thousands of feet thick.

The sun gives off energy by **radiation.** The sun's radiant energy travels to the earth through space in the form of visible light waves and invisible ultraviolet and infrared rays. Most of the visible light waves and the ultraviolet rays penetrate through the atmosphere and reach earth's surface. Infrared rays, on the other hand, are more often absorbed in the atmosphere or reflected back into space. Of all the energy that the earth receives from the sun, about one third is reflected back into space. The remaining two thirds warms the earth and the atmosphere and makes our planet habitable.

The sun's radiant energy is absorbed by the earth during a process called **insolation** from the words *"in*coming *sol*ar radi*ation."* Only a small part of insolation is soaked up by the atmosphere. Most of the insolation reaches the ground where it is absorbed and heats the surface.

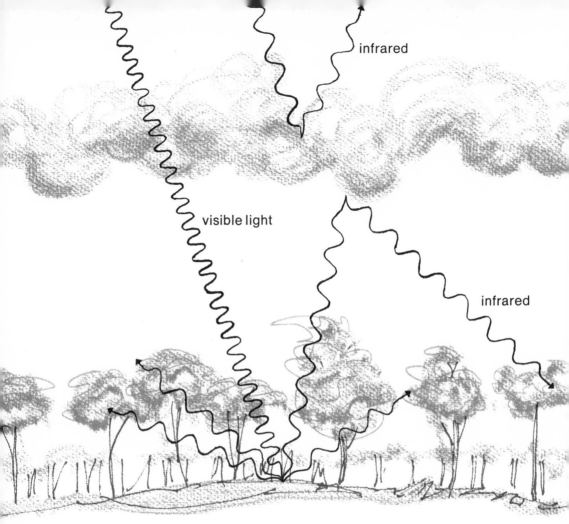

Greenhouse effect

The ability of the atmosphere to let light waves and ultraviolet rays through while absorbing infrared rays is called the "greenhouse" or "atmospheric" effect. It takes its name from the all-glass greenhouse used to grow plants. Light rays pass through the glass into the greenhouse, hit the ground, and are changed to infrared rays—the most effective heating rays. These changed rays cannot get out through the glass. As a result, heat builds up inside the greenhouse. The same sort of thing happens in the atmosphere.

Heat passes from the surface of the earth to the lower layers of the atmosphere and back again by **conduction.** Conduction occurs when a warm and a cold object come in contact. Heat flows from the warm object into the cold object. Sometimes the warmed surface of the land heats the air above it. At other times, when the land is cooler than the air, the air warms the land.

Some substances, such as metals, are good conductors of heat, but air is a very poor conductor of heat. If conduction were the only way heat could be transferred, only the bottom few feet of the atmosphere would be hot during the summer. Several feet above the ground, the air would be quite cold. Fortunately, heat transfer in the atmosphere takes place through movement of the air itself. We call that process **convection.**

You can see the effects of convection by putting some small pieces of tissue paper over a warm radiator. Air above the radiator is heated, expands, and becomes less dense. The warmed, lighter air moves upward, carrying along some of the tissue paper. When the air reaches the ceiling, it begins to cool and becomes denser. The denser air moves downward and across the floor toward the radiator. The circulation of air is called a convection current. Convection currents are found throughout the earth's atmosphere.

Many things determine the temperatures of a region. Perhaps the most important factor is the amount of solar radiation that reaches it. For example, insolation at the equator is about two and one-half times greater than at either of the poles. It comes as no surprise to learn that most of the earth's cold spots are in the Arctic and Antarctic.

But other places not far from the equator, such as Mt. Kilimanjaro, are covered with snow year-round. Kilimanjaro is a 19,000-foot mountain located in East Africa about 250 miles from the equator. On its high icy peaks, temperatures usually stay below freezing.

High-altitude balloon and rocket observations show that air temperature drops at a fairly regular rate upward to the tropopause. As mentioned in Chapter 2, the average rate of decrease in tempera-

Kilimanjaro, showing the snowline

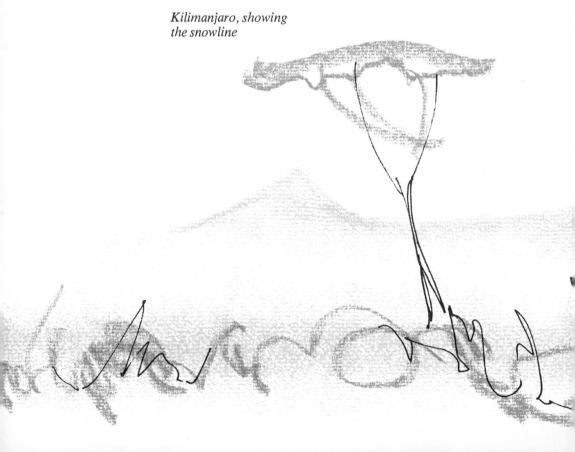

ture is about 3.5 degrees Fahrenheit for each 1,000 feet of altitude. The decrease of temperature with altitude is called the lapse rate.

On the tops of many high mountains, snow piles up faster than it melts or evaporates. Places like this are said to be at or above the snowline. The snowline is highest in equatorial regions and lowest in polar regions. Along the west coast of the United States, the snowline is at an altitude of about 5,000 feet. In polar regions, the snowline is at sea level.

Local features of a region also affect the temperature. Clouds, water vapor, dust particles and other substances in the atmosphere cut down the amount of radiation that reaches the earth. Thick clouds may cut insolation by as much as 80 percent. On the other hand, a dry clear atmosphere lets in most of the sun's rays.

The amount of radiation reflected from the ground also varies. Forests, for example, reflect less than 10 percent of the energy they receive. Concrete surfaces reflect about 35 percent, while newly fallen snow reflects as much as 90 percent.

Land warms up and cools off much more rapidly than water. You can feel this when you walk across the hot sand of a beach into the cooler water along the shore. Water takes longer to warm because waves and currents spread heat very rapidly throughout the water by convection. Land areas transfer heat downward very slowly by conduction. This keeps the land surface very warm on a summer day. Large bodies of water store a great deal of heat and release it slowly at night or during the winter. Land can't store much heat at the surface and becomes cold more rapidly.

For these reasons, yearly temperature ranges over land areas are greater than temperature ranges over oceans. Also, mid-continent regions have warmer summers and colder winters than coastal regions. South Dakota, for example, has much colder winters and warmer summers than Rhode Island.

Many other factors affect temperature readings. In the Northern Hemisphere, north-facing slopes of mountains and hills receive less sun than south-facing slopes. Snow may melt weeks earlier on slopes with a southerly exposure. The position of mountains and plateaus, valleys and plains, rivers and lakes, ocean currents and a host of other things influences local temperatures.

28

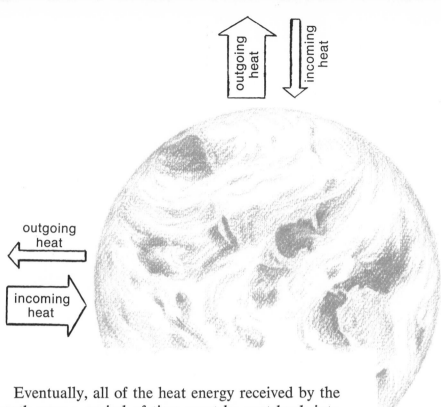

Eventually, all of the heat energy received by the earth over a period of time must be sent back into space. If too much energy was released, the earth would soon become very cold; if not enough energy was released, the earth would soon become very hot. Since the earth's average temperature remains at 57 degrees Fahrenheit, there must be an overall balance between incoming and outgoing energy. This is known as the atmospheric heat balance.

The low latitudes around the equator receive more heat than they radiate back into space. The high latitudes of the polar regions radiate more heat than they receive from the sun. So the surplus heat from the equatorial regions moves toward the polar regions where it escapes the earth. This vast exchange of heat between equator and poles is the key to the giant circulation patterns of atmosphere and oceans that make up weather and climate.

Hurricane Donna, photographed in Florida in September 1960, raged from Puerto Rico through the Florida Keys and up the coast of New England with winds that sometimes reached 180 miles an hour.

4 The Ways of the Winds

How simple it would be for weathermen to make predictions if the earth did not rotate on its axis. Imagine a planet that did not rotate, with a smooth surface free of mountains and other irregularities and with no water vapor in the air. Imagine an equator equally heated on all sides by a sun in the shape of a circular light bulb. Let's see what would happen under these conditions.

At the equator, the surface would be heated by the incoming radiation. The air in contact with the surface would be warmed, become less dense, and rise. At the poles, the air would be cooled, become denser, and settle downward.

31

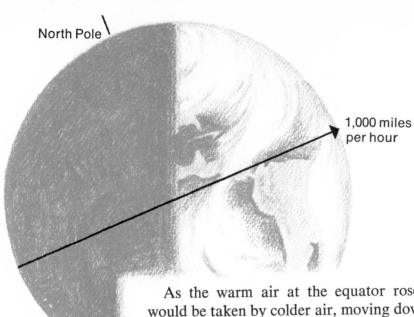

North Pole

1,000 miles
per hour

*The speed of rotation
at the equator*

As the warm air at the equator rose, its place would be taken by colder air, moving down from the poles. When it reached the equator, this air would also be warmed, rise, and flow toward the poles in the high troposphere. Over the poles, the air would cool, sink to the ground, and continue the same pattern. The basic circulation along the surface would be from the poles toward the equator.

But, alas for weathermen, the earth does rotate, only one side is heated at one time, the surface is irregular, and there is water vapor in the atmosphere. Let's see how these factors affect the circulation of the earth's atmosphere.

The earth makes one turn from west to east each day. Near the equator, the speed of rotation is about 1,000 miles per hour. That means the lands, the peoples, and the atmosphere around the equator are all moving at that speed. At the poles, the speed of rotation is much less. The difference in speeds causes a condition called the **Coriolis effect.**

You can show the Coriolis effect with a phonograph turntable, a piece of blank paper, scissors, a ruler, and a pencil. Cut the paper in the shape of a

32

circle and place it over the turntable. Revolve the turntable at its slowest speed. Hold the ruler over the rotating paper and point it to the center. With the pencil, try to draw a straight line on the paper, using the ruler as a guide. The line will always curve. The reason is that the outside of the turntable (like the equator) revolves at a faster speed than the inside spindle (like the poles). Since a turntable turns in a clockwise direction, the line will curve to the left. If you were looking down on the South Pole of the earth from out in space, you would see the earth turning clockwise, like the turntable. The result is that anything set into motion would curve toward the left.

In the Northern Hemisphere, the opposite is true. Any body in motion, such as the atmosphere, behaves as if it were being pushed to the right when you look in the direction of motion. In the Southern Hemisphere, the Coriolis effect shows up when bodies in motion, such as the atmosphere, seem to be pushed to the left.

The Coriolis effect, with other factors such as the irregular areas of land and water on the earth and the differing amounts of water vapor in the atmosphere, causes the circulation patterns of the atmosphere to be more complex than in our simple nonrotating model. These general patterns are sometimes called the earth's wind belts.

Doldrums

The **doldrums** are the belt of winds located around the equator. The winds are changeable, blowing from the north or the south toward the equator. They are usually light, gentle breezes. Most of the air motion is upward with little horizontal motion, giving rise to dead calms on the surface. The lack of strong, regular winds forced sailing ships of long ago to avoid this area. The word "doldrums" itself means dullness, low spirits—an apt description of the area.

Around 30 degrees north or south latitude (distance from the equator measured in degrees), the warmed air rising above the equator cools and settles back to the earth's surface. Because of the settling air, the latitude is one of great calms and few winds. The area is known as the **horse latitudes.** The name comes from the time when many sailing ships bound for America carried cargoes of horses. Becalmed ships often ran out of water and the horses had to be thrown overboard.

Trade winds

From the horse latitudes, sometimes called the subtropical high-pressure areas, winds move in two directions—toward the equator and away from the equator. The air moving back toward the equator appears to move westward because of the Coriolis effect. Because we name winds for the direction from which they come, the winds are called east winds. On both sides of the equator, the belts of winds blowing toward the equator are called the **trade winds.**

In the Northern Hemisphere, the winds are called the northeast trades. In the Southern Hemisphere,

34

they are called the southeast trades. The trade winds were named for the trade routes that sailing ships used in traveling through them. They blow steadily and dependably over the oceans at an average of 10 to 15 miles per hour.

From the horse latitudes, the winds moving away from the equator seem to be coming from the west because of the Coriolis effect. These belts of winds are called the **prevailing westerlies.** In the Northern Hemisphere, they are southwesterlies and in the Southern Hemisphere they are northwesterlies. The westerlies are highly variable. At times they are mild and calm. But at other times they blow at gale force. The westerlies are not even constant in direction. They may blow from any point of the compass—westerly just being the most common. Sailors call these latitudes "the roaring forties."

Prevailing westerlies

The westerlies cover the zones where most of the earth's population lives—the so-called "temperate zones." The name is a bad one. The only thing temperate about the zones is that a great deal of heat is exchanged here between the equator and the poles. But if you live in New York or Chicago, you know that it can seem like the North Pole one day and the equator another day. The changing patterns of the winds in this zone make it the hardest in which to predict the weather—as you know if you've ever been misled by a prediction for fair weather and been caught in the rain.

Cold and stormy winds blow from both poles toward lower latitudes. These are known as the **polar easterlies.** In the Northern Hemisphere, cold

Polar easterlies

35

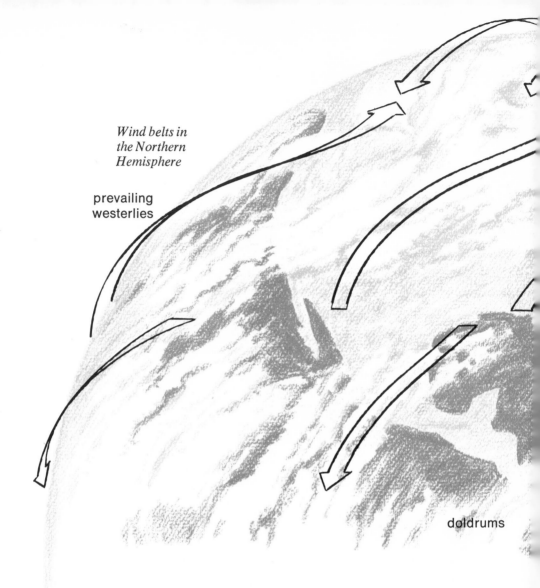

Wind belts in the Northern Hemisphere

prevailing westerlies

doldrums

masses of polar air often move southward into the westerlies during the winter. Along the shipping routes in the North Atlantic and North Pacific, high waves and gusty winds make the going rough.

The basic circulation pattern of the atmosphere is subject to many variations and changes. For example, air is heated over warm land areas such as

36

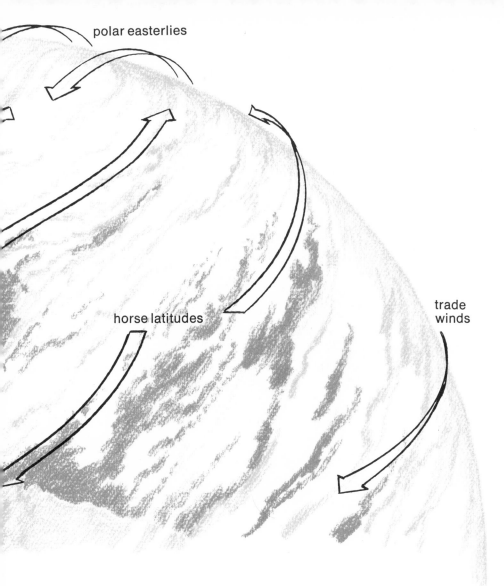

polar easterlies

horse latitudes

trade
winds

deserts, cooled over large stretches of ice and snow, warmed by some ocean currents and cooled by other ocean currents, and greatly changed by being lifted over mountain chains.

The climate of India illustrates the importance of surface features on wind patterns. The Himalaya Mountains block the northern approaches of India,

37

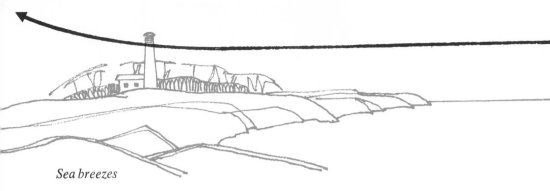

Sea breezes

while oceans surround the rest of the country. In the winter, the mountains at first act as a temporary barrier to the cold winds of the north. Little or no rain falls. But when enough cold, dense air piles up, it pours over the mountains covering large areas of India. This produces a high-pressure area over the land. Winds blow toward the warmer, less dense low-pressure areas of the Indian Ocean. In the summer, heat builds up in the atmosphere until the heated air rises above the slopes of the mountains. When it does, air currents drawn in from the surrounding oceans bring in heavy rains. These seasonal winds are called **monsoons.** India has a rainy monsoon from June to November and a dry monsoon from December to May.

Monsoon effects happen every day along coastal regions. These "daily monsoons" are called land and sea breezes. During the daytime, the sun warms land areas more quickly than nearby oceans or other waters. Warmed air over the land rises, leaving a low-pressure area. Cooler air above the water sinks and becomes an area of higher pressure. At the earth's surface, winds blow from high-pressure areas toward

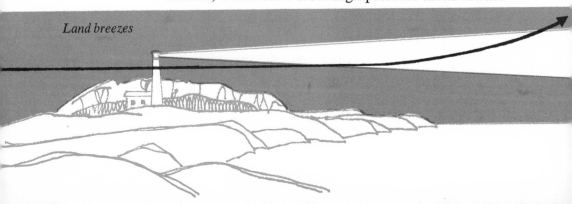

Land breezes

Mountain breezes

low-pressure areas. So during the day, winds blow from surrounding waters toward land. These winds are called **sea breezes.**

During the nighttime, conditions are reversed. The land cools off more rapidly than the water. Air pressure becomes higher over the now-cooler land than over the comparatively warmer water. Winds, called **land breezes,** blow from land areas toward the water. Land and sea breezes often develop along the shorelines of lakes as well as along ocean coasts. In many parts of the world, fishermen put out to sea with a land breeze in the early morning and return with a sea breeze in the afternoon.

Other examples of daily wind shifts are mountain and valley breezes. During the night, colder, heavier air from the mountain top pours down the slopes into the valley below. These strong winds are called **mountain breezes.** During the day, the air over mountain slopes warms up more rapidly than the air over the valley. The cooler valley air presses downward forcing the warmer air up the slopes. These winds are called **valley breezes.** They usually blow with less velocity than mountain breezes.

Other kinds of local winds can be caused by mountains. They are known by a host of different names in different countries: the chinook of the Rocky Mountains, the foehn of the Alps, the zonda of the Andes. Winds that come about as a result of local surface features are called **orographic winds** (from the Greek *oros,* mountain). For example, the

Valley breezes

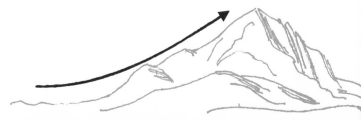

chinook, foehn, and zonda blow across mountains, lose their moisture, and blow hot and dry into the valleys below. A fast-moving chinook can dry up a blanket of snow in a valley in a few hours.

Other famous orographic winds are the cold bora of the Balkans, the equally fierce mistral of France, the dry sirocco of the Mediterranean coast, and the hot simoom which causes sandstorms in the deserts of Africa and Asia.

All of these winds are surface winds. But there are also winds higher up in the atmosphere. They, too, follow regular patterns. In the upper air from about 20 degrees latitude almost to the poles is a system of westerly winds blowing in a complete circle around the earth. At lower latitudes is a system of easterly winds blowing around the equator.

The upper-air westerly winds tend to form curving paths that move toward the poles or equator at different times. Along these paths are narrow bands

jet stream

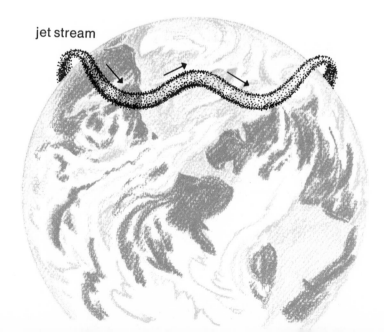

in which winds reach velocities of up to 300 miles per hour. The wandering currents of high-speed winds are the **jet streams.** In the Northern Hemisphere, the jet stream forms the line between the colder air of the north and the warmer air of the south.

Pilots flying eastward use the jet stream to increase their speed and save fuel. The jet stream blows at altitudes of twenty to forty thousand feet. It is about four miles deep and about three hundred miles wide. The path of the jet stream changes from day to day and from season to season. The location of the jet is an important aid in predicting the weather.

The picture of the earth's wind systems is far from complete. But we know that winds blow from warmer areas to cooler areas. And the winds are a major factor in distributing the sun's heat evenly around the world.

Eight major storms over the Northern Hemisphere. This picture was built up from a series of satellite photographs taken in a single day.

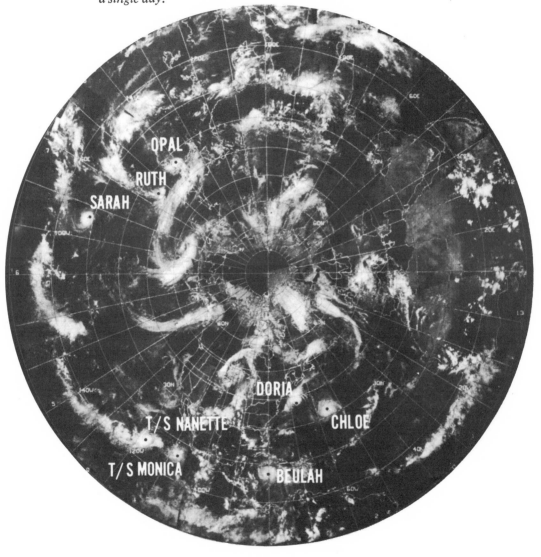

5 The Atmosphere in Motion

North America is the site of a continuous battle. The battle is between large bodies of air called **air masses.** Like opposing armies, air masses push each other back and forth across the continent. Air masses are separated from each other by sharp boundaries. The boundary line between the different bodies of air is called a **front.** The weather of a region changes every time a front and the air mass behind it pass over. The battle of the air masses plays an important part in the frequent changes in our weather.

Air masses form over many different regions of the earth. When the air remains over one region for several days, it takes on some of the properties of the area. For example, an air mass forming over central Canada becomes dry and cold, while an air mass forming over the Gulf of Mexico becomes moist and warm.

An air mass may sit over a region and grow till it reaches over a thousand miles in diameter. Eventually currents in the upper air and the earth's rotation start the air mass moving. Air masses travel thousands of miles from where they form. As each new air mass appears over a section of the country, it brings a change in wind patterns, temperature, and humidity.

Weathermen identify each air mass by a set of

43

initials that describe its properties. Air coming from cold, northern regions is called "P," polar air. Air coming from the warm south is called "T," tropical air. The letter "m" stands for humid air coming from maritime (ocean) regions and the letter "c" for dry air coming from continental areas. Combinations of these letters stand for the four types of air masses that mainly influence United States weather.

From the central forests and plains of Canada comes a cP (continental polar) air mass. It sweeps down into the United States from the northwest bringing cold and dry air. In the summer, this air mass brings relief from the muggy weather of the eastern half of the country. In the winter, it brings in a cold snap. It can bring the cold reaches of winter as far south as the orange groves of Florida and the cattle ranches of Texas.

Often, a cP air mass from the north pushes against an mT (maritime tropical) air mass that was born over the Gulf of Mexico or the Caribbean Sea. Air masses from tropical ocean areas are warm and moist. An mT air mass usually comes in on southerly winds bringing the kind of uncomfortable summer weather about which people say, "It's not the heat, it's the humidity!"

Sometimes mP air from the North Pacific pushes into the Northwestern States bringing steady rains and fogs. From the North Atlantic, a different mP air mass brings in the well-known "northeaster," cold, steady rain with strong winds that drenches New England and the Middle Atlantic States.

Much less frequently, a cT air mass from Mexico

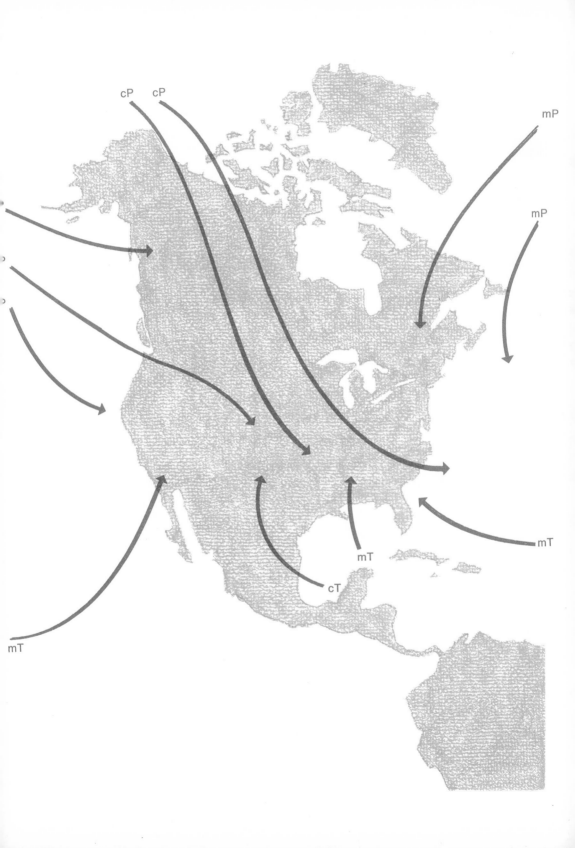

cold air

Cold front

pushes its way into the Southwestern States. This air is warm and dry.

Weathermen also use two other letters. These indicate the temperature difference between an air mass and the surface over which it passes. If the air mass is colder than the surface, a "k" for the German word *kalt* (cold) is used. If the air mass is warmer than the surface, the letter "w" is used. Cold, dry air that passes over a warmer surface is labeled cPk, while warm, moist air passing over a colder surface is labeled mTw. If temperatures of the air mass and the surface are about the same, these additional letters are not used.

There are usually several different air masses moving in a generally easterly direction (pages 120–121) across the United States at any one time. Fronts, where two air masses meet, have a very gradual vertical slope at the leading edge. The slope differs in different air masses. In diagrams of fronts the slope is always exaggerated so it will show up, but in reality even a steep front slopes no more than one mile vertically for forty miles horizontally.

46

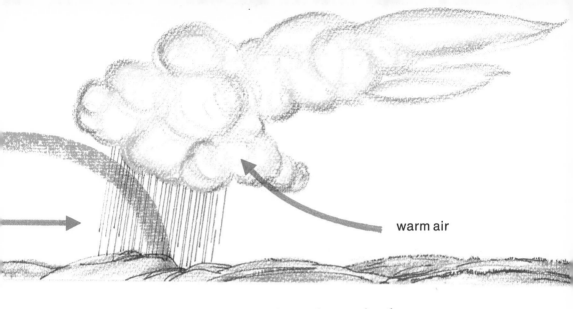

warm air

The arrival of a front signals a change in the weather. Sometimes the change is a small one, such as cool air replacing colder air. But at other times the change is more dramatic, as when cP air pushes out mT air. Then warm, humid weather is replaced by cool, dry weather. Often, the arrival of a front is accompanied by some kind of precipitation, either rain or snow.

Weathermen can locate a front by observing where sharp changes in weather occur. Temperatures are often quite different on each side of a front. The wind blows from different directions and with different velocities on each side. Humidity measurements are different, too. Certain cloud types form with each kind of front.

Fronts are named according to the motion of the air masses behind them. If a cold air mass is advancing as a warm air mass retreats, the boundary line between the masses is called a **cold front.** The cold air pushes as a sort of wedge under the warm air forcing it to rise. A cold front is usually steeper than a warm front. As a result, the rapidly rising warm air

47

warm air

Warm front

cools quickly. Towering cloud systems form ahead of the front, and a narrow band of showers and thunderstorms accompanies it.

Cold fronts move faster and arrive more dramatically than warm fronts. There is little advance cloudiness. As the front nears, clouds build up quickly and it begins to rain. Temperature falls, and the wind shifts around to a northerly direction and increases in velocity. A drop in air pressure often announces the oncoming cold front. But as the front passes over, air pressure rises again. Rainfall may continue for a few hours after the passage of the front. After the rain stops, the sky usually clears and the incoming cold air mass determines the weather.

Warm air advances while cold air retreats along a **warm front.** Warm fronts have more gradual slopes than cold fronts. The warm air may rise only a few thousand feet for every hundred miles in advance of the ground location of the front. This great mass of rising air may extend for a thousand miles in advance of the ground front. Thin, high-flying cirrus clouds—mare's-tails—often appear 24 hours in ad-

48

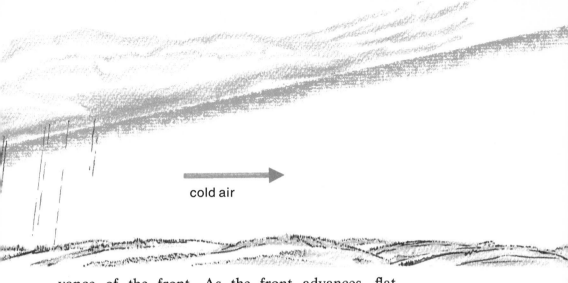

cold air

vance of the front. As the front advances, flat, thick layers of stratus clouds turn the sky a dull gray. Rain and drizzle are continuous and extend over a wide area. In wintertime, snow, sleet, or freezing rain often occurs when raindrops fall from the warm air and pass through the cold air below.

When the warm front passes, air temperature rises and the rain ends. The wind shifts but not as sharply as at the passage of a cold front. Air pressure falls as the front passes and then rises as the air mass comes through. Once more, weather is determined by the incoming air mass.

Fronts move across the United States at an average velocity of about 20 to 30 miles per hour. Usually they move faster in winter than in summer. The difference in velocity depends upon the difference in air pressure between the air masses. Some air masses are dense and heavy. They are called **highs,** or **anticyclones.** Other air masses are regions of low pressure. These are known as **lows,** or **cyclones.**

A typical low develops along the line where cold polar air is in contact with warmer, lighter air to the south. A wave motion forms along the front and

warm air

cold air

Occluded front   begins to move from west to east. The wave creates a leading warm front where the warm air is pushing northward and a trailing cold front where the polar air pushes southward. Between the two fronts lies the warm air forming a low. Because of the Coriolis effect, winds in the Northern Hemisphere blow in toward the center of a low in a counter-clockwise direction. Lows in the United States have an average diameter of about 1,000 miles.

As a low continues to move, the trailing cold air pushes rapidly into the lower-pressure warm air. Often, the faster-moving cold front overtakes the slower-moving warm front. When the air mass behind the cold front reaches the one in advance of the warm front, the warmer air between the fronts is pushed aloft. This is called an occlusion (closing in) and the front is known as an **occluded front.**

There are two different kinds of occluded fronts, but both types usually cause the rain or snow that comes with either warm or cold fronts or even with a mixture of the two. As the occlusion continues, the air masses mix together and the low disappears.

Sometimes fronts slow down and stop moving. They are then known as **stationary fronts.** Because the warm air mass is still rising above the cold air mass, a stationary front develops the gently sloping

50

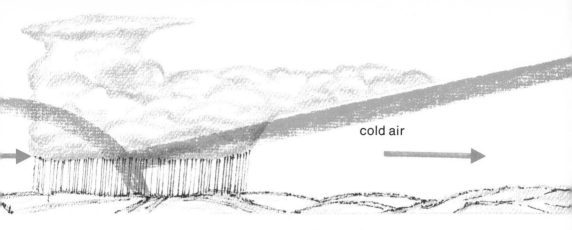

cold air

shape of a warm front. The weather of a stationary front is then similar to that of a warm front. But the rainy weather lasts longer than it does during the passage of a warm front. Stationary fronts may start to move in either direction and, depending upon which air mass is advancing, become either a warm front or a cold front.

Large masses of heavy air form highs, or anti-cyclones. In a high, air pressure is highest at the center and decreases outward. Winds blow outward and clockwise in the Northern Hemisphere. Highs do not have fronts or lines of sharp wind shifts. They are more stable than lows and are usually associated with fair weather systems. A high may range from a few hundred miles in diameter to over 2,000 miles in diameter. Usually, highs travel much slower than lows. A large high can bring fair weather to a region for many days.

Important high-pressure areas around the United States include the Bermuda high and the Pacific high over oceans, and the Canadian high and Siberian high over continental areas. During the winter, the cold, dry highs influence our weather more than the warmer, moist highs found over the oceans. During the summer, coastal areas are more influenced by the highs found over the oceans.

51

6   Water in the Air

Almost all of the water on our planet is in oceans, lakes, rivers, ponds, and in the ground. Only a tiny trace is found in the atmosphere. Yet this small amount of water vapor plays a more important part in weather than any of the other gases of the air. Rain, snow, fog, humidity, clouds, frost, hail, sleet—

all are water in one form or another.

The amount of water in the air varies from one place to another and from one time to another. It decreases with altitude. Over half of the total moisture in the atmosphere is found below a height of two miles. Generally, air over tropical oceans contains more moisture than air over colder waters or over land areas.

53

Water exists in the air in any or all of the three states of matter. It appears as a solid in the form of snow, sleet, or hail; as a liquid in the form of rain, clouds, and fog; and as a gas in the form of invisible water vapor. It can easily change from one state to another, and this change always involves heat. The constant changes in the amount of water in the atmosphere and the state that it is in greatly influence the weather.

Water passes into the air from the surface of oceans and lakes, glaciers and ice fields, from moist ground, and by transpiration from the leaves of plants. The change from liquid water to water vapor is called **evaporation.** A special kind of evaporation, from ice or snow directly to water vapor, is called **sublimation.**

When water evaporates, it absorbs heat from its surroundings. That's why you feel cool when you come out of the water after bathing. The evaporating water takes heat from your body. The speed of evaporation depends upon the temperature of the water. The higher the temperature, the more quickly water evaporates. Water also evaporates more quickly into dry air than into moist air. On a windy day you feel even cooler after bathing because the wind keeps changing the layer of air touching your skin.

The change from water vapor to liquid water is called **condensation.** When water vapor condenses, it returns some heat to its surroundings. The amount of heat it gives up is equal to the amount it absorbed when it evaporated. It slows down the rate of cooling in the atmosphere and is one of the main sources of heat energy for weather changes.

When water vapor condenses, it forms small droplets of water. The droplets take shape around tiny solid particles in the air. These tiny particles are called condensation nuclei. Most of them are tiny bits of chemicals that absorb water. If enough water droplets form, you can see them, first as haze, then as clouds or fog as the amount increases.

Besides condensing and evaporating, water can change its state by **freezing** and **melting.** When water freezes, it changes from a liquid into solid ice. When ice melts, it becomes liquid water. And once again, heat is involved in the change. Heat is absorbed by the water when ice melts and released when water freezes. This helps to explain why the air around a pond is somewhat warmer when the pond freezes than the general temperature of the area.

Water freezes at a temperature of 0 degrees Centigrade, or 32 degrees Fahrenheit. However, it may not freeze until it reaches a lower temperature if other materials are dissolved in it. The amount of water can also lower the freezing point.

The amount of water vapor that air can hold depends upon the temperature of the air. If you raise the temperature of the air, it can hold more water. If you lower the temperature, it can hold less water. When air at a given temperature holds as much water as it can, it is said to be **saturated.** When you take a hot shower, the air in the bathroom is likely to be saturated. The water droplets covering the bathroom mirror show that some of the water taken up by the air must leave it so that more water can evaporate into it.

Weathermen are interested in the amount of water vapor actually in the air at a given temperature compared to the amount it can hold when saturated. This relationship between the two amounts is called the **relative humidity**. For example, a relative humidity of 50 percent means that the air contains half as much water vapor as it can possibly hold. Relative humidity is measured with an instrument called a hygrometer (see page 107).

Saturated air is at 100 percent relative humidity. The temperature at which saturation occurs is called the **dew point.** The dew point depends upon the amount of water in a given volume of air. When air is cooled below its dew point, some of the water vapor in it must condense. For example, suppose that on a summer day the air temperature is 80 degrees Fahrenheit and the relative humidity is 75 percent. At night, the temperature drops down to 68 degrees. This is below the air's dew point, and it can no longer hold all the water vapor it contained at 80 degrees Fahrenheit. Some of the water vapor condenses into visible water—drops of dew on the grass or early morning mists or clouds. As the temperature rises the next day, the air can hold more water vapor and the morning mist evaporates.

One way to understand all this is to think of the air's capacity to hold water vapor as a glass jar. The size of the jar depends on the temperature of the air: the higher the air temperature, the bigger the jar. The jar can be filled with a certain amount of water. If the jar is half full, that would be 50 percent relative humidity. A full jar would be at its dew point, 100 percent humidity. If the temperature falls, the jar would become smaller. It would be able to hold less water, and some would spill over the side.

Most clouds occur when air rises and its temperature falls below its dew point. Some of its water vapor condenses to form clouds. Rapidly rising air currents usually make upward-growing, puffy clouds. Clouds resulting from a gentle rise will spread out in layers.

Clouds are grouped in families according to their height, appearance, and composition—water droplets or ice crystals. There are four groupings: high clouds, middle clouds, low clouds, and clouds with vertical development. Their heights are measured from the surface over which they appear, not from sea level.

Three cloud names occur in all the groupings. Cirrus (meaning curling) are thin, ice crystal clouds. Stratus (meaning spread out) are layers of clouds. Cumulus (meaning mounds) are piled, woolly clouds. When two of the names are combined, as in stratocumulus, the cloud has some of the properties of both names. Nimbus refers to a rain cloud, and alto means a cloud form that is high in altitude. Fracto before a cloud name is used to describe clouds that are torn by the wind. Fractocumulus, for example, are fair weather clouds that are broken up by strong winds.

Cirrus clouds are thin, wispy clouds sometimes called mare's-tails. They often seem to form a ring or halo around the sun or moon. The halos result from the bending of light rays by the multitudes of ice crystals that make up these clouds.

Cirrostratus are veil-like clouds. These clouds are so thin that blue sky or bright stars show through them.

Cirrocumulus clouds appear as patches of white arranged in rows. They look like a rippled sandy beach.

High clouds include cirrus, cirrostratus, and cirrocumulus. They are formed of ice crystals and are found from 20,000 feet up to the beginning of the tropopause. Cirrus clouds usually mean fair weather for 20 to 30 hours followed by rain or snow.

59

Altocumulus clouds are long rolls of thin clouds arranged in parallel rows. They often cover the entire sky.

Middle clouds usually occur at altitudes of 20,000 feet down to about 6,500 feet. The two main types are altostratus and altocumulus. Often, altostratus and altocumulus change into each other. If the wind is steady from the northeast, rain or snow follows these clouds in 10 to 15 hours.

Altostratus clouds are blue-gray in color and the sun shines through them as if through frosted glass.

Stratocumulus clouds form low, gray layers in groups or waves. When the groups can no longer be made out, the clouds have become stratus.

Low clouds include stratocumulus, stratus, and nimbostratus. These clouds are found from 6,500 feet and on down.

Stratus clouds form a foglike layer that does not rest on the ground. These dark, low clouds give us gray, drizzly days though sometimes the rain may be heavy.

Nimbostratus are thicker rainy- or snowy-day clouds. Usually precipitation is much heavier from nimbostratus than from stratus.

Cumulus clouds appear as puffy, dome-shaped tufts of cotton. They are usually seen on fair and sunny days at any time of the year.

Vertical development clouds occur in rapidly rising air and form cumulus or cumulonimbus types.

Cumulonimbus clouds are the familiar flat-topped thunderhead clouds. At times they tower to 60,000 feet or more. They produce heavy rain or hail showers, often along with lightning and thunder. These most often occur on hot summer days when there are strong rising air currents.

Fog hides the far side of this bridge.

Fog results when water vapor condenses into tiny droplets close to the ground. The droplets are so small that even a slight movement of air keeps them aloft. A fog can be thought of as a cloud whose base touches the ground.

Radiation fog (ground fog) forms when moist air

is cooled by contact with the ground overnight. The ground cools by radiating heat during the night. If there is no wind only dew or frost forms. But winds will mix the cooler bottom air with the warm moist air higher up. The moisture condenses, forming a fog. These commonly form in valleys and hollows around ponds and streams during autumn nights. The fogs are thickest at daybreak but are usually quickly burnt off by the morning sun. Radiation fogs do not form at sea because water doesn't lose so much heat at night. In polar lands, radiation fogs form of ice crystals and are sometimes called "diamond dust" because of the way they glitter in the light.

Advection fog occurs when winds carry moist air over a cold surface. It's often seen at sea where air from a warm ocean current such as the Gulf Stream flows across colder ocean waters. Upslope fog forms when warm, moist air rises up a sloping plain or hill and condenses. This is a common type of fog on the eastern slopes of the Rocky Mountains. Westerners sometimes call it a "Cheyenne fog." Mixing fog takes place in the frontal zone between masses of warm, moist air and cold, moist air. When you see your breath on a cold day, it is similar to a mixing fog.

"Sea smoke" or steam fog sometimes appears over cold ocean waters. Evaporating quickly from the ocean, the water condenses into a column of fog that reaches heights of up to one mile. This kind of fog is somewhat different from the others because it results from quick evaporation, not from cooling.

Telephone lines weighted down with ice

7   Precipitation

Water falling to the earth in a liquid or solid form is called **precipitation.** The most common kinds of precipitation are rain, drizzle, snow, sleet, and hail. Dew and frost are not considered precipitation, though we shall mention them later in this chapter.

Precipitation falls from clouds—but not all clouds. Many people know the kinds of clouds that bring precipitation. "It looks like it's going to rain," they say. But sometimes it doesn't rain. And that is a mystery that weathermen tried to solve for many years. Why doesn't it rain when all the conditions seem to be right?

Part of the answer was found in a strange new scientific theory. In order for most rain to fall, said the Swedish scientist Tor Bergeron and the German scientist Walter Findeisen, it must begin as snow.

Raindrops are thousands of times larger than cloud droplets. The important question is how and why these tiny droplets come together to form the heavy raindrops that fall from the clouds.

67

The Bergeron-Findeisen theory says that rain falls when thick clouds build up high enough in the atmosphere for ice crystals to form among the water droplets. Water vapor in the clouds condenses onto the ice crystals. The crystals become heavier and begin to fall. As they fall, they bump into other droplets and combine with them. If they fall through cold air, they reach the ground as snow. If they pass through warm air, they melt to fall as rain.

Not all rain begins in this way. Rain over tropical areas probably results from strong upward air currents. These twisting winds drive cloud droplets together. The heavier droplets fall, collide with other droplets, and grow larger. Eventually they grow heavy enough to fall as rain.

Drizzle is somewhat different from rain. Drizzle droplets are small and close together. They seem to float in the air. Drizzle falls from low-hanging stratus clouds. Often, drizzle brings fog and poor visibility. In some places, drizzle is called mist.

Snow begins in the same way as most kinds of rain. Ice crystals begin to grow in the upper levels of vertically developed clouds such as cumulus and cumulonimbus. Water vapor crystallizes onto the cold crystals. Finally the crystals grow heavy enough to begin falling. If the air is cold all the way down, they reach the ground as snow.

Snowflakes are usually six-sided crystals or stars. No two snowflakes seem to be alike and each is geometrically beautiful. Catch a few snowflakes on a black cloth and examine their shapes with a magnifying lens. At very low temperatures, snow is harder

68

and more grainy. At warmer temperatures, snow-flakes clump together in soggy masses of wet snow.

A snowstorm or snow blizzard can dump many inches of snow on the ground. But if the snow is melted, it usually contains only a small amount of water. Under most conditions, eight to twelve inches of snow is equal to about one inch of rainwater.

Sometimes snow crystals melt on the way to the ground and become rain, then pass through a cold layer of air and freeze into hard pellets of ice. These frozen raindrops are called **sleet.**

Sleet is not the same as the freezing rain which may cover roads and streets with a slippery, hard coating. This kind of sheet ice is called **glaze.** Glaze forms when rain hits cold surfaces on the ground and freezes on contact. If glaze keeps forming for some time, it is called an ice storm. Trees and telephone

69

Cross section of a hailstone

and power lines are often damaged by the weight of the ice during these storms.

Hail forms in thunderstorms during warmer weather. If you slice a hailstone through its center, you will find it made up of alternate layers of snow and ice. Large hailstones have many layers. Scientists explain that hailstones are tossed upward and downward by great gusts of rising and falling air in thunderclouds. Hailstones fall into a warm lower layer of cloud, collect a coating of water, and then are swept up into a colder layer of cloud and frozen.

The more powerful the thundercloud, the more rides for the hailstone, and the larger they grow. Finally, they become so large that they are no longer held up by the winds and fall to the ground. Sometimes, several hailstones freeze together and fall as a large chunk of ice.

The worst hailstorms appear over the midwest sections of the United States during warm weather. They often cause great damage and may even kill people who are caught in the open. A hailstone which fell at Potter, Nebraska, in 1928 weighed one and one-half pounds. It was as big as a grapefruit.

Dew and **frost** do not fall down; they form directly on cooled surfaces on the ground. During clear, still

70   *Possible path of a hailstone in a thunderhead*

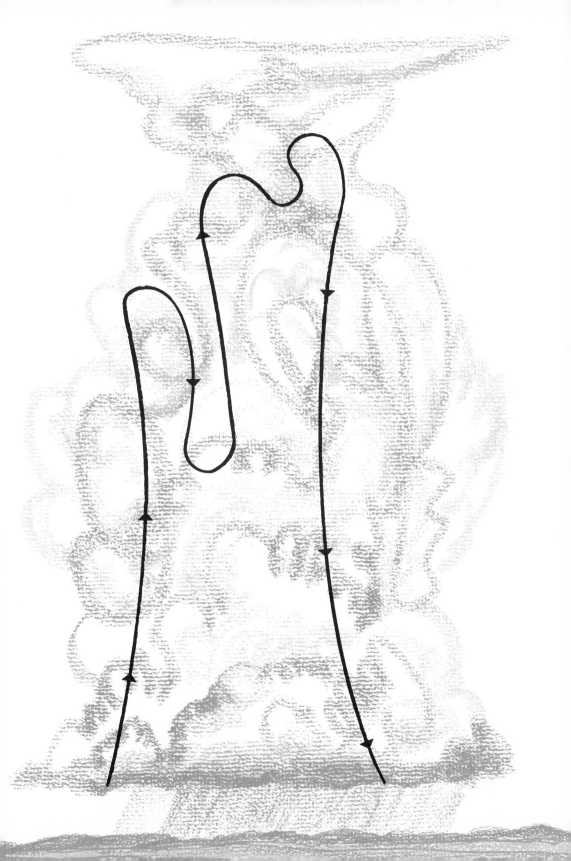

nights, grass, shrubs, and other objects cool off by radiation very quickly. If their temperature falls below the dew point of the surrounding air, moisture condenses on them in exactly the same way droplets collect on the outside of a pitcher of ice water.

If the temperature at which the water condenses on a surface is below the freezing point, then frost forms instead of dew. On a cold winter night, you may see feathery frost crystals form on the inside of your windowpane. Usually, the morning sun quickly evaporates dew and frost.

Average yearly rainfall varies greatly from one region to another. The western coasts of continents in the middle latitudes are areas of heavy rainfall. For example, the coastal regions of British Columbia and Washington State have over 80 inches of rainfall per year. Other places have even more. Cherrapunji in northeast India averages 426 inches per year. Mt. Waialeale in Hawaii averages 460 inches per year.

Contrast these areas with Death Valley, in California, which averages about one inch per year. For some parts of desert regions no appreciable rainfall has ever been observed.

Why should rainfall vary so much? Rainfall occurs where air is cooled below its dew point by rapidly rising and expanding. The warmer the air the more moisture it contains, the higher it rises, and the more it rains. The rainy areas of the earth are those places where moist air frequently rises in large amounts.

The wind belt called the doldrums fits all these

conditions well. In the doldrums, warm, humid air is constantly pushing upward to form huge cumulo-nimbus thunderheads. Rainstorms are a daily occurrence. Within the doldrums lie the dense tropical rain forests of the Amazon, the Congo, Borneo, New Guinea, and Sumatra.

Other regions of heavy rainfall are found on the windward sides of mountains. Here air is forced to rise over a mountain barrier. If the air is warm and moist, heavy showers and thunderstorms result. The rainy, windward slopes of the Olympic and Cascade mountains of the West Coast are examples of this type of rainfall. Even in the dry areas of the southwestern United States, mountain ranges and high plateaus receive rainfall on their windward sides during summer months.

Areas that receive very little rain are regions where air descends rather than rises. When winds blow downward, air is warmed by compression. Little precipitation occurs. This warm descending air creates deserts in some regions.

The horse-latitude wind belts fit these conditions. In both the Northern and Southern Hemispheres, the 30 to 35 degree latitudes are areas of high pressure, where dry descending air creates waterless lands such as the Sahara and the Great Australian Desert.

The sheltered sides of mountains are also regions of dry, descending air. The Great Basin Desert of Nevada located on the lee side of the coastal mountain ranges is an example. Other dry regions are found in the middle latitude, high-pressure wind belts and in the cold polar highs.

73

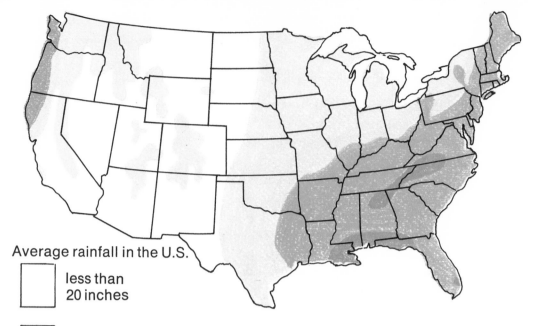

Average rainfall in the U.S.

less than
20 inches

20-40
inches

40-60
inches

over 60
inches

Most places in the world fall between the extremes of dry desert and wet rain forest. From about 10 inches of rainfall per year to about 60 inches per year is the range for most continental areas. New York, London, Rome, Tokyo, and many other major cities have average yearly rainfalls in this range. For cities in colder regions, average rainfall includes melted snow water.

Of course, yearly averages are not the whole story. Whether the total rainfall comes down over many days or in a few heavy showers is of great importance. The number of precipitation days per year along with the yearly average is important to any region's climate.

In the doldrums wind belt, rainfall is almost daily. Even the pattern of rain is fairly regular. Usually, the mornings are clear with just a few puffy cumulus clouds. By noon and mid-afternoon, the cumulus

74

clouds have built up into towering cumulonimbus thunderheads. The downpour comes in the late afternoon. After an hour or two, the rain stops, the sky clears, and then it will be fair again until the next day.

Precipitation in temperate regions may be seasonal (the monsoon effect) or occur when frontal systems pass by. Other kinds of precipitation depend on local conditions such as the direction of the wind and the type of air mass.

Precipitation can sometimes be unbelievably heavy. Here are some record-breaking downpours:

During one minute on July 4, 1956, Unionville, Maryland, had 1.2 inches of rain.

During a 42-minute period on June 22, 1947, Holt, Missouri, had 12 inches of rain.

During a period of one week in June 1931, Cherrapunji, India, had 131 inches of rain.

During 1861, Cherrapunji had 1041 inches of rain. Compare your local area records for rainfall with that of Cherrapunji and you will get some idea how much rain 1,000 inches—83 feet—a year is.

Weather on a Rampage

8

It's hard to believe that the warm, sunny Caribbean Sea is one of the breeding places of the killer storms called **hurricanes.** Yet some of the most dangerous hurricanes are born there.

A hurricane is a large low-pressure area similar in some respects to the "lows" of the mid-latitude regions. Low-pressure areas are called cyclones. A hurricane is a tropical cyclone. Cyclones have winds blowing in toward the center: counter-clockwise in the Northern Hemisphere and clockwise in the Southern Hemisphere. Usually cyclones are accompanied by areas of heavy precipitation.

But a hurricane is something special. The United States Weather Bureau describes a hurricane as "a large revolving storm originating over tropical ocean waters with winds of 74 miles per hour or more blowing counter-clockwise around the center." Hurricanes are known under different names in different parts of the world. In the tropical waters of the western Pacific Ocean, they are called typhoons. Off northwest Australia, the storms are called willy willies. In the Indian Ocean, they are called cyclones. But no matter what their names, they are universally feared.

In the Caribbean hurricanes usually occur in late summer or autumn. They first start as weak low-pressure areas. As they grow, they pick up energy from the abundant moisture in the warm air over the ocean. Hurricanes get their whirling motion from the Coriolis effect as they move northward. Their usual path is northwestward and then northeastward, but many hurricanes move in unpredictable ways.

Hurricanes can be as small as 25 miles across, but most are from 100 to 600 miles. They tend to increase in size as they move to the north. Unlike other lows, hurricanes have no fronts or wind shift lines. Air pressure drops quickly toward the center of a hurricane. The great pressure difference accounts for the high winds. Surprisingly, the central 5- to 30-mile portion of a hurricane, the "eye," is a place of calm winds and sunny skies. In the eye, descending air currents make a clear and warm region, while the storm rages all around.

Hurricanes often travel at speeds of 10 to 20 miles

per hour, but they can speed up or slow down unpre-
dictably. They will travel a path of perhaps 1,000
miles before blowing themselves out at sea. Hurricanes are tracked by plane, by radar, and by weather
satellite. The United States Weather Bureau issues
hurricane advisories, giving information about a
storm's location, force, and movement. A hurricane
warning is issued when a storm is expected to hit a
coastal area in 24 hours or less. Hurricanes are given
girls' names in alphabetical order each year. Every
four years, the list of names is repeated. Since 1900,
about five hurricanes each year have appeared off
the east coast of the United States.

Hurricanes have high winds that flatten houses,
blow down trees, and hurl debris through the air.
Hurricane wind force is at least 74 miles per hour,
but many hurricanes carry wind speeds in excess of
100 miles per hour, with sudden gusts as high as 250
miles per hour.

*Eye of the hurricane
is seen as a dark spot
to the right of the +.*

79

A twister approaches Topeka, Kansas, on June 8, 1966.

As a hurricane approaches the coast, it causes the sea level to rise above normal heights with giant, wind-driven waves and strong currents. The high waves also cause coastal damage even before the hurricane moves inland.

One such storm tide was caused by "Betsy" in 1965. From September 7 to 10, Hurricane Betsy struck the Florida Keys and Miami with 150-mile-per-hour winds, then swept across the Gulf of Mexico to hit New Orleans. Despite advance warnings of this killer from the sea, 74 people died and property damage was estimated at more than one billion dollars.

Hurricanes are not the only destroyers from the sky. An even more violent storm is the **tornado.** On the average, a tornado, or twister, follows a path only a quarter of a mile wide and 16 miles long. Yet the dark funnel of a tornado can cause immense

80

destruction. It can uproot solid buildings and other large objects and hurl them for hundreds of yards. In 1931, according to a weather bureau report, a tornado in Minnesota "carried an 83-ton railroad coach and its 117 passengers 80 feet through the air."

In the United States, tornadoes most often occur in the Midwest during the spring and early summer. They cover a much smaller area than hurricanes. Tornadoes usually develop along frontal lines separating warm and cold air masses. Nobody has ever accurately clocked the winds inside a tornado funnel, but they are thought to rotate at speeds of 200 to 300 miles per hour. Tornadoes are often accompanied by thunderstorms, hail, and lightning.

Tornadoes do their damage through the combination of whirling high-speed winds and the partial vacuum in the center of the funnel. The winds rip at the outsides of buildings at the same time that the vacuum causes the higher pressure inside the building to explode the walls and windows outward.

Each year the Midwest—particularly the "tornado belt" of Iowa, Kansas, Arkansas, Oklahoma, Mississippi, Illinois, Indiana, and Missouri—is visited by an average of 600 tornadoes. Some years there are many more. On one violent day in 1965, the Midwest was hit by thirty-seven tornadoes. Two hundred and seventy-one people were killed and hundreds of millions of dollars' worth of property was destroyed by the savage twisters. Since the early 1950s, deaths from tornadoes have averaged over 100 each year.

A waterspout

Tornadoes at sea are called **waterspouts.** Waterspouts are usually smaller in diameter than land tornadoes but they behave in the same way. A waterspout picks up some ocean water when it makes contact with the surface, but its funnel mostly contains condensed water. Waterspouts are rarely as destructive as land tornadoes.

Because of a tornado's unpredictability and short life, the Weather Bureau cannot give long advance warnings of them as they do with hurricanes. They do broadcast tornado watches to alert people to the possibility of tornadoes in a particular area during a certain period of time. Tornado warnings are issued when twisters have actually been sighted either in person or on radar.

Thunderheads are another example of weather's more violent moods. Cumulonimbus clouds—thunderheads—develop over heated surfaces of land or sea. The warmed areas transfer their heat to the air above them and it becomes a rising air current called a **thermal.** As a thermal rises, it passes through cooler, drier air. The moisture in the thermal then condenses and forms a puffy cumulus cloud.

Thermals continue to rise in the middle of the cloud, causing the cloud to grow above the freezing level. Snow crystals form in the upper levels of the cloud, fall, and become raindrops. The falling rain causes downdrafts in the frontal, lower parts of the cloud. The updrafts in the back and top of the cloud and the downdrafts in the front build the cloud to heights of 40,000 feet or higher. Now a towering cumulonimbus, the thunderhead often produces hail and lightning as well as heavy rain.

Thermals in a cumulus cloud ... developing into a cumulonimbus

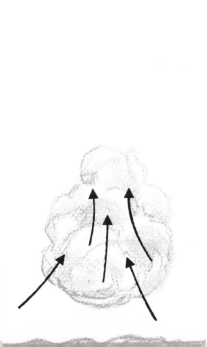
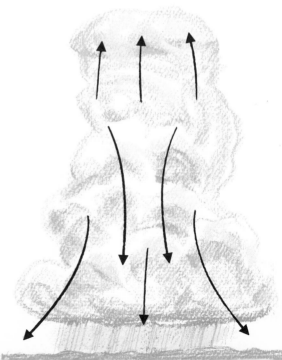

Scientists are not exactly sure how thunderstorms produce lightning. They know that electrical charges are important in the formation of raindrops and ice crystals and that lightning often follows precipitation.

Thunderheads usually have a concentration of positive charges in the upper part and a large negative charge surrounding a positive area in the lower part. Electricity discharges as lightning to the ground, to another cloud, or within the same cloud.

There may be more lightning around than you think. Scientists say that about 1,800 thunderstorms occur at different spots around the earth at any one time. They estimate that around the world lightning strikes the ground 100 times each second. Despite the old saying that lightning never strikes twice in the same place, lightning can and does. For example, the Empire State Building in New York City has been struck a dozen times within the space of a few minutes.

Each year in the United States an average of 600 people are killed and 1,500 are injured by lightning. The death toll is higher for lightning than for tornadoes or hurricanes. Property damage as a result of lightning-started fires is estimated at over $100 million a year.

Thunder is the sound of lightning. The sound is produced when air expands suddenly because of the great heat of a lightning flash and then cools and contracts rapidly. The little snap you get from an electric spark is a kind of miniature thunder. Thunder is impressive but not dangerous in itself.

Still other kinds of destructive weather are bliz-

84

zards, ice storms, and dust storms. **Blizzards** are large winter storms combining high winds, low temperatures, poor visibility, and a lot of snow over a long period of time. According to the Weather Bureau, a "severe" blizzard has winds of over 45 miles per hour, temperature under 10 degrees Fahrenheit, and great snows.

Blizzards occur nearly every year in the northern and middle sections of the United States. The remarkable blizzard of 1888 remains the standard by which other blizzards are measured. For four days during March of that year, winds averaged 20 to 25 miles per hour, with gusts of 50 to over 70 miles per hour. Snowfall averaged 40 inches or more over southeastern New York and southern New England. New York City, Washington, Philadelphia, and Boston were paralyzed. In New York City alone

Ice storm

more than 200 people died, thousands were injured, and property damage was widespread.

Blizzards are still with us. In December of 1962, gale-force winds and zero temperatures combined to produce one of the worst blizzards of the century throughout New England. A new snowfall record was set for Maine, when 40 inches fell in 24 hours. In places, drifts piled up to over fifteen feet. Traffic was halted, schools and businesses closed, and over a dozen deaths resulted from the storm.

Ice storms are not as dramatic as blizzards, but they still cause much property damage. Ice storms result when rain freezes as it hits the ground or other surfaces. The frozen rain forms a coating of ice or glaze. The ice coating ranges from a thin shield to about one inch thick.

Some ice storms, however, deposit much thicker

coatings. In 1961, layers of 8 inches were reported on telephone wires in northern Idaho, and 6-inch deposits were reported in Texas in 1940 and New York in 1942. The heavy accumulation of ice snaps telephone and power lines, trees, and bushes. Weathermen say that a 50-foot-high evergreen tree may be coated by as much as 10,000 pounds of ice during a severe ice storm. The ice coating on streets and highways makes driving hazardous. Most deaths from ice storms result from traffic accidents caused by slippery conditions.

Whatever else may be said about ice storms, they enclose the landscape in layers of beautiful crystal. Not so **dust storms.** There is little good you can say for them. Dust storms result from strong winds picking up loose soil, carrying it to great heights and great distances, and dumping some of it along the way. In desert regions, dust storms or sandstorms are

common during periods of high winds. In other areas dust storms occur during droughts.

During the drought years of the early 1930s, huge, brown dust storms swept across the Great Plains of the United States and Central Australia. Millions of tons of topsoil and other earth materials were carried away, leaving great eroded areas on the surface of the land.

Oklahoma recorded 180 dust storms in just two years during the '30s. During those drought years, hundreds and thousands of farms in the Southwest were turned into uninhabitable wasteland. Thousands of people packed their belongings and departed for other places. These migrants were called "Okies" because so many of them came from Oklahoma's "dust bowl." Even today, the Great Plains of the United States bear the scars of the dust storms of the '30s.

89

9 Climates: Big and Little

We call the long-term weather of any particular place climate. The climate of a region is made up of such things as temperature, type and amounts of precipitation, winds, humidity, storms, and clouds. Climate is influenced by latitude and altitude, by the location of mountains and bodies of water, by prevailing winds and ocean currents. Of course, weather changes from day to day and from month to month. So climate is really the sum total of all the weather of a region.

Yet even the climate of a region may not be able to tell us what kind of weather to expect each day. Within a large region there may be many small areas that have their own special climates. For example, large cities often have temperatures higher than surrounding areas. One side of a mountain may be very rainy but the other side quite dry. Shorelines of large bodies of water have climates different from those of areas only a short distance inland.

Climatologists, scientists who study climates, have methods of classifying different types of climate.

91

The Western Rif in northern Morocco has a Mediterranean climate. This type of climate is found between west coast tropical deserts and marine west coast climates. In the summer, desert conditions take control and bring severe drought, but the temperature is moderate because the ocean is near. In winter, there is lots of rain.

Rainforest in Puerto Rico

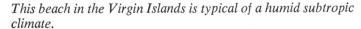

This beach in the Virgin Islands is typical of a humid subtropic climate.

Humid continental is a changeable climate found in the eastern half of North America and large parts of Europe and Asia. There is no land mass in the Southern Hemisphere large enough to have this type of climate.

Marine climates are usually found along the west coasts of continents. Here, a redwood forest meets the sea in northern California.

The subarctic climate zone contains the northern forests of spruce and fir, seen here, and a more open woodland called the taiga.

No trees grow on the arctic tundra.

The polar icecap in Greenland "calves" huge icebergs along the crevasse lines seen here. The wall of ice at this point is about 200 feet high.

The Himalaya Mountains in Nepal have a highland climate.

Climates change just as weather does, but at a much slower rate. The earth used to be generally a much warmer place than it is now. In fact, studies of plant and animal fossils (hardened remains of living things) seem to show that 90 percent of our planet's past average temperatures were higher than the average temperature today. Fossils of tropical plants have even been found in the polar regions.

However, there have been periods of cold lasting a few million years (not very long by geological standards). Sometimes, climate changes occur over shorter time spans. For example, glacier evidence, deposits of plant pollen, and other ways of dating past climates seem to show that climates have been generally cooling for the past thousand years, until perhaps the nineteenth century. Since then, weather records seem to show a general warming trend. But even this may not continue. Since 1948, glaciers on Mount Ranier and Mount Baker have been growing, and average winter temperatures appear to be decreasing slightly.

The main difficulty in predicting what will happen is that no one is sure of what causes climatic changes. Some scientists think that the amount of carbon dioxide in the atmosphere causes climate changes. Other scientists believe that changes in the earth's rotation or shifts in the tilt of the axis influence the climate. Still others believe that variations in solar radiation or the amount of dust in the atmosphere are responsible.

Not all climates stretch over vast ranges of land and water. There is another kind of climate that exists in just a small area. This might be the sides of a valley or a hill or the north and south walls of a house. Climate a few inches above the ground is often different from spot to spot. These miniature climates are called **microclimates.**

People have been adjusting to microclimates for a long time, though perhaps not realizing it. A house built on the leeward side of a hill needs much less heating than a house built on the windward side or on the crest of the hill. A row of trees can serve as a windbreak and have the same effect. Different kinds of grass seed have been developed for lawns on the shady side of a house as well as for sunnier locations. Many people wear light-colored, loose clothing in warm weather to create a cooler microclimate for themselves.

Sometimes we control microclimates to an even greater extent. When we burn fuel to heat a house or when we cool it with an air conditioner, we are making a microclimate. The inside of a car, train, or airplane is a controlled microclimate. An electric blanket, a hair dryer, a hot bath, a cool spray of water are all ways of making a microclimate.

Not all microclimates that man produces are intentional, however. Whenever a field is plowed, a tree uprooted or planted, a house or a road built, a car engine or a barbecue fire started, microclimates are produced. And while each of these microclimates has only a tiny effect on the weather, enough of them put together have a great effect indeed.

For example, a large city influences its own local climate. The blacktop streets and roofs that absorb

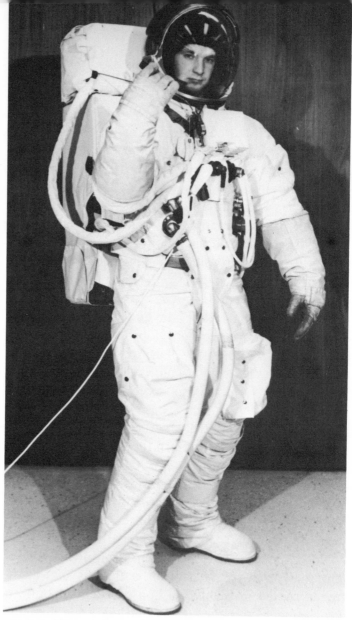

A microclimate is created inside a spacesuit.

heat, buildings that give heat, and the lack of trees and other plants usually result in a city being several degrees warmer than the surrounding countryside. This warmed air sometimes combines with smoke

100

and other pollutants and produces smog or some other irritating conditions. Over many cities a bluish-gray haze of smog hangs dully in the atmosphere.

Air a few inches above the earth's surface usually changes temperature more rapidly than air at a height of several feet. This is particularly true in hot regions. For example, ground temperatures in the desert may reach 170 degrees Fahrenheit in the afternoon and drop to about 60 degrees Fahrenheit at night. This is an extreme daily temperature range of over 100 degrees. Small animals and young plants living at ground level must adapt to these conditions.

All microclimates are not equally as changeable. The type of soil or rock, the plant cover, the presence or absence of nearby bodies of water, as well as the locality, affect the microclimate. Still, most microclimates show a wide variety of climatic changes.

At the lowest levels, wind direction is often different from that of the wind currents usually shown on a weather map. The features of the surroundings, such as shape and size, influence the wind direction. You can easily see this by watching the motions of leaves or paper on a windy day. Air currents, counter-currents, and whirlpools develop in and between buildings, trees, and other surface features.

Climatology and micro-climatology are important branches of science, not only for what they tell us about the weather, but also because they are important in agriculture, city planning, house building, air pollution, field studies in biology, and many other areas.

101

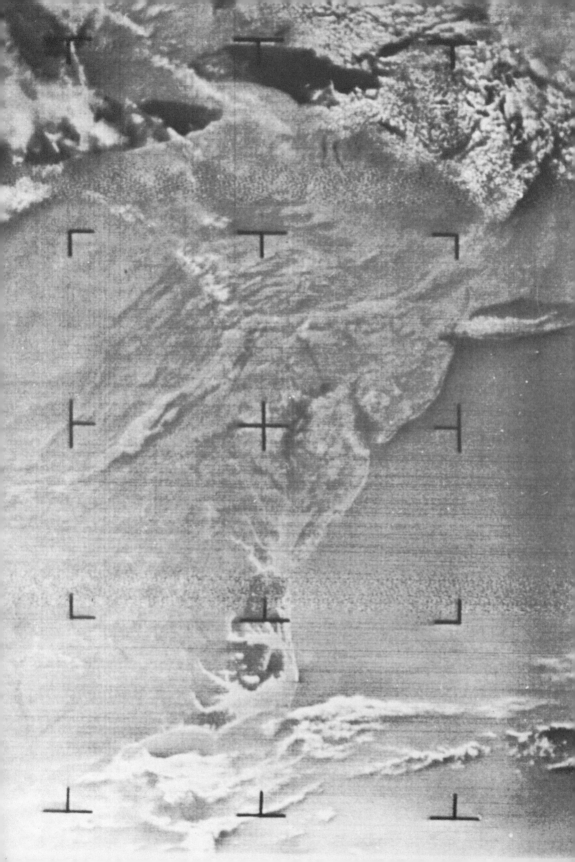

Clouds over the eastern part of the United States, photographed from 430 miles high by the Nimbus 1 weather satellite

Watching
and Measuring
10   the Weather

Predicting the weather is somewhat like predicting the outcome of a ball game. The more you know about what the ball teams did before, the more likely your prediction will be accurate. In the same way, the more a weatherman knows about what the weather did before, the more likely his prediction will be accurate. Of course, in both cases predictions sometimes turn out to be wrong. But without background information, a prediction is no more than a guess.

To make predictions accurately, weathermen observe and measure changing conditions in the atmosphere which are related to the weather. Instruments for making these observations are continuously being developed and improved. But regardless of the instruments used, the weatherman still needs to know about the same basic weather factors: air pressure, wind force and direction, air temperature, humidity and dew point, precipitation, and type and amount of clouds.

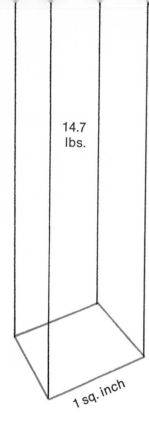

14.7
lbs.

1 sq. inch

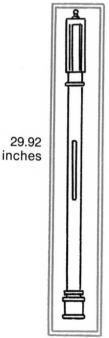

29.92
inches

Barometer

Air pressure is a measure of the weight of the atmosphere at a particular time and place. Changes in air pressure play a very important role in predicting weather. For example, a drop in air pressure often signals the coming of rainy weather. High pressure, on the other hand, often means fair weather. This is because "highs" usually have falling dry air at their centers.

A column of air one square inch in area reaching from sea level to the top of the atmosphere weighs about 14.7 pounds. The weight of this air pressing down can support a column of mercury 29.92 inches high in a glass tube. Because of this, scientists say that normal air pressure at sea level is 29.92 inches.

The instrument used to measure air pressure is called a **barometer.** The earliest kinds of barometers used mercury to measure pressure. Nowadays, another kind of barometer, an aneroid barometer, is often used. Aneroid means "without liquid." An aneroid barometer has a metal can from which most of the air has been removed. When air pressure around the can increases, the can is forced in a little bit. When air pressure decreases, the can pushes out a little bit. These small movements are shown on a dial. The dial is marked in inches in the same way as a mercury barometer.

Weathermen all over the world now use a unit of pressure called a **millibar.** Millibars are metric units. About 34 millibars are equal to one inch of mercury. Normal sea-level pressure of 29.92 inches of mercury is equal to 1013.2 millibars (abbreviated as mb).

104

Air pressure shows a rapid decrease with altitude. For example, the pressure at 18,000 feet is only half the pressure at sea level. But at sea level, pressure rarely drops lower than about 29 inches (982.1 mb) or rises higher than about 31 inches (1050.0 mb).

A barograph is an aneroid barometer that makes a continuous record of atmospheric pressure. A sheet of graph paper is fastened on a cylinder which is turned by a clockwork motor. The cylinder makes one complete turn in a week. A pen records changes on the graph paper so that a glance is enough to show whether air pressure is rising, falling, or steady.

The force of the wind is measured in miles per hour by an **anemometer.** Most weather observation stations use cup anemometers. The wind is caught in the cups and causes them to turn. The stronger the wind, the faster the cups turn. The speed of turning is shown on a dial from which readings may be taken.

Wind direction is usually measured with the familiar **wind vane.** The push of the wind on the vane causes it to point into the wind. Wind direction is given as the direction from which the wind is blowing. For example, a vane pointing *toward* the west shows a west wind.

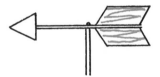

Wind vane

Air temperature is measured by a **thermometer.** Thermometers work on the principle that substances expand when heated and contract when cooled. Liquid thermometers use either alcohol or mercury as the expanding material. Mercury is a heavy, silvery liquid that becomes a solid at about −39

105

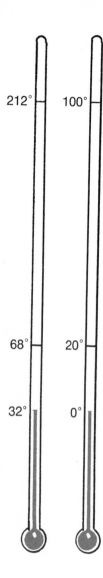

212° 100°

68° 20°

32° 0°

degrees Fahrenheit. Below this point, mercury contracts too slowly to be easily visible. Because of this, mercury thermometers are not used in extremely cold climates. Alcohol is a colorless liquid, with a freezing point of about −200 degrees Fahrenheit. It is usually colored red or blue to make it visible. While it is less accurate than a mercury thermometer, an alcohol thermometer can be used in colder locations. Non-liquid thermometers usually use metal coils or springs that react to changing temperatures.

An instrument that makes a continuous record of temperatures on graph paper is called a thermograph. Thermographs use the same type of inside clock gears as do barographs. A maximum and minimum thermometer records just the highest and lowest temperatures during any period of time. They contain devices which stay at the highest and lowest temperatures reached.

The two most common thermometer scales are the **Fahrenheit** and the **Centigrade** or **Celsius.** The reference points on a thermometer are called degrees. A **degree** (°) is a definite fraction of the difference in temperature between the freezing point of pure water and its boiling point. On the Fahrenheit scale, used mostly in the United States, 32° is the freezing point and 212° is the boiling point. On the Celsius scale, used in Europe and in most laboratories throughout the world, 0° is the freezing point and 100° is the boiling point. Because of this difference, $1° C. = 1.8°$ (or $\frac{9}{5}$) F. To change Celsius temperatures to Fahrenheit or vice versa, you can use these formulas: $C = \frac{5}{9}(F - 32)$ and $F = \frac{9}{5}C + 32$.

106

Relative humidity is measured with an instrument called a **hygrometer.** One kind of hygrometer is the psychrometer or wet-and-dry-bulb thermometer. This is a set of two thermometers. The dry thermometer gives the temperature of the air. The wet one has a piece of cloth fastened around the bulb, which the weatherman wets before he takes a reading. Evaporation of water from the cloth causes the temperature of the wet thermometer to fall. The drier the air, the more the evaporation and the more the cooling. The difference in the temperatures gives the relative humidity which can be checked on a specially worked-out table.

Another kind of hygrometer is called a hygrograph. Hygrographs work on the principle that some substances get longer in humid air and shorter in dry air. Human hair is very sensitive to moisture, so many hygrographs use a bundle of human hairs. These are attached to a pointer that traces a mark on a sheet of rotating graph paper. Dew point (see page 57) is either measured directly by an instrument known as a **dewcell,** or it can be figured out by using hygrometer readings and a table.

Precipitation is measured by a **rain gauge.** This is usually a large can with a funnel on top. The funnel leads into a smaller can inside. The inner can has only one-tenth the area of the funnel top, so the rain water is ten times deeper in the inner can. This makes it easier to measure the rainfall to a small fraction of an inch. Tipping-bucket gauges or weighing gauges can measure and record rainfall electrically.

Snowfall and other solid forms of precipitation

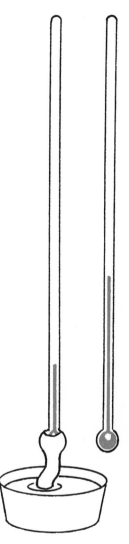

Wet-and-dry-bulb hygrometer

107

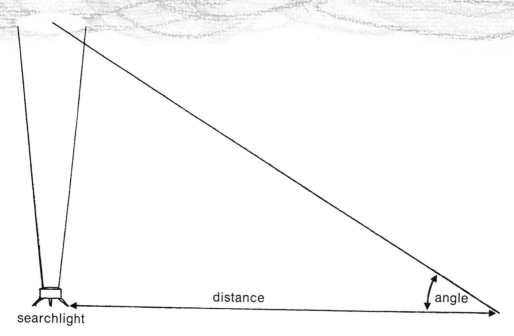

distance

angle

searchlight

Ceilometer

can be measured in two ways. A measuring stick is
sometimes used. The stick is pushed into the snow on
level ground in several locations. The average of
three or more different places is used as the depth of
snow. Another way is to melt the snow collected in a
rain gauge and measure the water. Depending on the
kind of snow, about ten inches of snow is equal to
one inch of water.

Cloudiness is usually measured by the fraction of
the sky covered by clouds. An experienced observer
can estimate this by eye quite accurately. The state
of the sky is given in this way: if the number of
tenths of cloud cover ranges from 0 to 3, it is said to
be clear; from 4 to 7, partly cloudy; over 7, cloudy.

Height of the cloud base, or ceiling, is measured
by eye observation or by an instrument called a
ceilometer. A ceilometer projects a spot of light on a
cloud base. A detector scans the beam of light and

sends an electrical message of cloud height that is recorded on a graph.

By themselves, observations taken at the surface are not sufficient for accurate forecasting. The atmosphere extends hundreds of miles above the ground. Information about these upper layers is of great importance to weathermen. During the last part of the nineteenth century and first quarter of the twentieth, kites carrying weather instruments were used to explore the air to about 10,000 feet. But the kites presented a number of problems, one being that the kites could be flown only in good weather when winds were just strong enough. Airplanes were then used for a number of years, but they also could not be used in stormy weather.

In 1937, radiosonde observations were introduced. Radiosonde observations (Raobs) are radio soundings of the upper air. Instruments are carried into the upper air by hydrogen- or helium-filled balloons and their readings transmitted to earth by radio. A radiosonde can reach heights of over 100,000 feet. When the balloon bursts in the low pressure of the upper atmosphere, a parachute opens and slows the radiosonde's descent.

Radiosonde observations are taken two to four times daily at over 100 weather stations throughout the Western Hemisphere. The data from these observations are sent to weather bureaus around the world. Radiosondes are also tracked automatically from the ground. The tracking gives the direction and speed of the winds through which the radiosonde is passing. These observations are called rawinsondes.

109

Sometimes a large balloon carrying many weather instruments is designed to float at a given altitude for several days. This is called a transosonde. Transosondes move with the wind and send back much information about upper wind patterns.

A newer system uses balloons that float at the same height for many months. Most weather balloons are made of stretchable rubberlike neoprene and expand until they eventually break. Constant-level balloons are made of a light, nonstretchable material called mylar. They remain the same size and will only rise to a certain level. One such balloon in the GHOST system (standing for Global Horizontal Sounding Technique) stayed aloft for over 190 days and made 17 trips around the Southern Hemisphere before sinking to the ground. Weathermen hope eventually to have as many as 1,000 balloons circling the earth at different altitudes.

Observations by **weather satellite** began on April 1, 1960, with the launching of *Tiros 1*. The *Tiros* satellites from above took pictures of clouds. These pictures were invaluable in detecting hurricanes and watching weather patterns develop. New satellites in the TOS system (Tiros Operational Satellite) store data on magnetic tape and send it back to Earth as they pass ground stations. ESSA 2 (Environmental Survey Satellite) takes cloud pictures every few minutes for transmission to ground stations.

An even newer system of satellites called ATS (Applications Technology Satellites) was started in 1966. This type of satellite is designed to remain at

110

An ATS *satellite*

the same position over the earth's surface. The camera in ATS-1 can show the beginning, the development, and the ending of cumulus clouds as small as one mile in diameter.

The World Meteorological Organization (WMO), a member agency of the United Nations, has set up a program called the World Weather Watch. The United States is represented by the administrator of the Environmental Science Services Administration (ESSA) which includes the Weather Bureau. The aims of the World Weather Watch are to constantly observe the earth's entire atmosphere, to transmit weather information on modern equipment to all nations, and to improve weather forecasting.

With most of the world's nations sharing in the task of watching the weather, perhaps man will one day succeed in understanding the ever-changing patterns of weather and climate.

111

Equatorial weather picture built up from ESSA satellite photographs

Weathermen share their information. These machines receive charts and photographs sent from other stations.

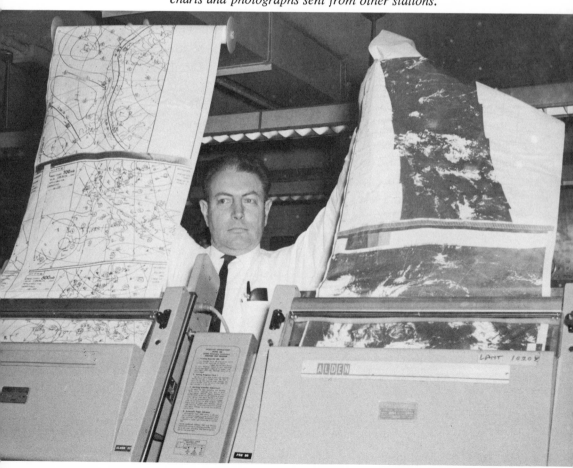

A meteorologist at ESSA's National Hurricane Center studies a built-up photograph of a storm.

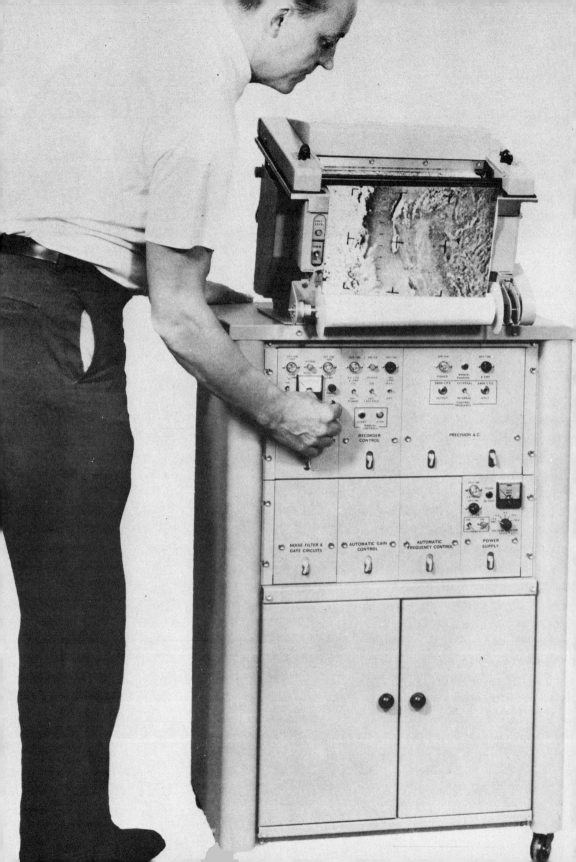

The new U.S. Air Force-type Automatic Picture Transmission Recorder is small, but it can instantly print photographs and maps showing a million square miles.

11 Tomorrow's Weather Today

"Probable nor'-east to sou'west winds, varying to the southard and westard and eastard and points between; high and low barometer, sweeping round from place to place; probable areas of rain, snow, hail, and drought, succeeded or preceded by earthquakes with thunder and lightning."

—Mark Twain, Speaking before the New
England Society on December 22, 1876

Weather forecasting has changed greatly since Mark Twain's time. Nowadays the United States Weather Bureau delivers short-range forecasts that are accurate about 85 percent of the time. Yet weathermen still make errors in their forecasts.

Everyone can remember at least one occasion when the forecast was for fair, sunny skies but the rains came. The trouble is that every time the Weather Bureau makes a mistake, everybody knows about it.

The Weather Bureau faces a difficult job in forecasting. At any one time there may be thousands of different kinds of local weather across the United States. One spot may have rain while another spot just a few miles away may be sunny. The constantly shifting atmosphere behaves in an unpredictable way. While many weather changes can be predicted beforehand, other changes give no advance warning.

Accurate forecasting is made possible by a knowledge of approaching weather patterns. To gain this knowledge, thousands of weather stations around the world, ships at sea, airplanes, and weather satellites send reports of current weather conditions into forecasting centers such as ESSA's National Meteorological Center in Maryland. Here, banks of computers run through the millions of bits of weather data and, in less than two hours, come up with predictions and weather maps that are teletyped to weather bureaus all over the country. Local weathermen interpret the maps and other data to make forecasts for their own sections of the country.

Studying a series of weather maps is a good way to see how weather patterns move. The circles on a weather map represent weather stations. Information gathered at each station is printed around the circle in figures and symbols. These show the kind of clouds, the ceiling, the temperature of the air, the dew point, the direction and velocity of the wind, the

116

air pressure and whether it's rising or falling, and the precipitation. The circle is white if the sky is clear, half black if the sky is partly clouded, or all black if the sky is completely overcast.

Lines, called **isobars,** are drawn to connect places having the same air pressure. The number on an isobar gives the barometric pressure in inches of mercury or in millibars. Isobars help weathermen locate high- and low-pressure centers which are then labeled. Using the positions of "highs" and "lows" as well as other data, the weatherman next draws in toothed lines that represent fronts. Areas of precipitation are shaded and other special information such as **isotherms** (lines of equal air temperature) may be added.

This basic weather map, called a **synoptic weather chart,** gives a summary of the weather at the surface. Synoptic observations for use in the map are taken at the same times throughout the world. Because so much information must be transmitted in such a short time, each station sends in its observations in the form of a code. The coded messages are translated and plotted on the synoptic map.

One principle upon which forecasts are based is that in the United States weather patterns move in a generally easterly direction. This is part of the planetary circulation belts of the earth's atmosphere. "Highs," "lows," and fronts are carried along and usually show an eastward movement from day to day. However, the speed of the eastward movement and its movement north or south varies.

Predicting the speed and direction of fronts and

An ESSA laboratory

This machine draws weather charts.

pressure systems is only part of the problem. Weathermen must still forecast what temperature changes will occur, whether there will be precipitation and if so how much, the humidity, cloudiness, and other weather features. It's easy to see why forecasts are sometimes inaccurate.

An actual weather forecast is made by a team of forecasters. Surface and upper-air charts, radar and weather satellite photos, and past weather maps that are similar to the current situation are all consulted. Computers and the use of mathematical formulas all combine to produce forecasting charts which give the surface locations of pressure areas, fronts, and upper-air conditions for the next 24 to 48 hours. Using these charts, a local weatherman with long experience in a particular area is usually able to make an accurate local forecast.

Forecasts by the Weather Bureau include information on frontal and air-mass movements, expected storm data, temperatures, precipitation, cloudiness, wind movements, humidity, and special conditions. Daily weather forecasts are issued four times each day with special reports as conditions warrant. A daily weather map is also issued in the morning.

Short-range forecasts for 12 to 36 hours in advance are the most accurate. Extended-period forecasts of from 5 days to 30 days in advance are more likely to be in error. In fact, accurate detailed forecasts for longer than three days in advance are still not possible.

The United States Weather Bureau performs a number of other services besides giving the daily

119

20 16 12 04

24

48
Seattle

48
Portland

24

43
Great Falls

Calgary

M

08

52
Winnipeg

00

Bismarck

37
Rapid City

L

08

50
Minneapolis
St. Paul

R

43
Boise

39
Casper

48
North Platte

54
Des Moines

L
Chi

44
Salt Lake City

R

40
Denver

R

53
Kansas City

81
St. Louis

43
Reno

52
San Francisco

59

20

Los Angeles

04 00 L

L

55

Oklahoma City

Little Rock

77
Albuquerque

73
Phoenix

17
Fort Worth

16

12

Scale of Miles

08

04

66
Galveston

12

L

08

Scale of Miles

| 0 | 100 | 200 | 400 | 600 | 800 |

EXPECTED WX MAP
FOR EARLY
WEDNESDAY MORNING

COLD FRONT	WARM FRONT	STATIONARY FRONT	OCCL FRO

○ CLEAR ◐ PARTLY CLOUDY ● CLO

Ⓡ RAIN Ⓢ SNOW Ⓕ FO

Ⓣ THUNDERSTORMS Ⓩ FREEZING RAIN

Ⓜ MISSING DIRECTION OF WI

🌀 HURRICANE

WEST WIND EAST

WIND SCALE
Miles Per Hour ○ Calm ○ 1-4 ○ 5-8 ○ 9-14 ○ 15-20 ○ 21-25 ○ 26-

TUESDAY APRIL 15 1969

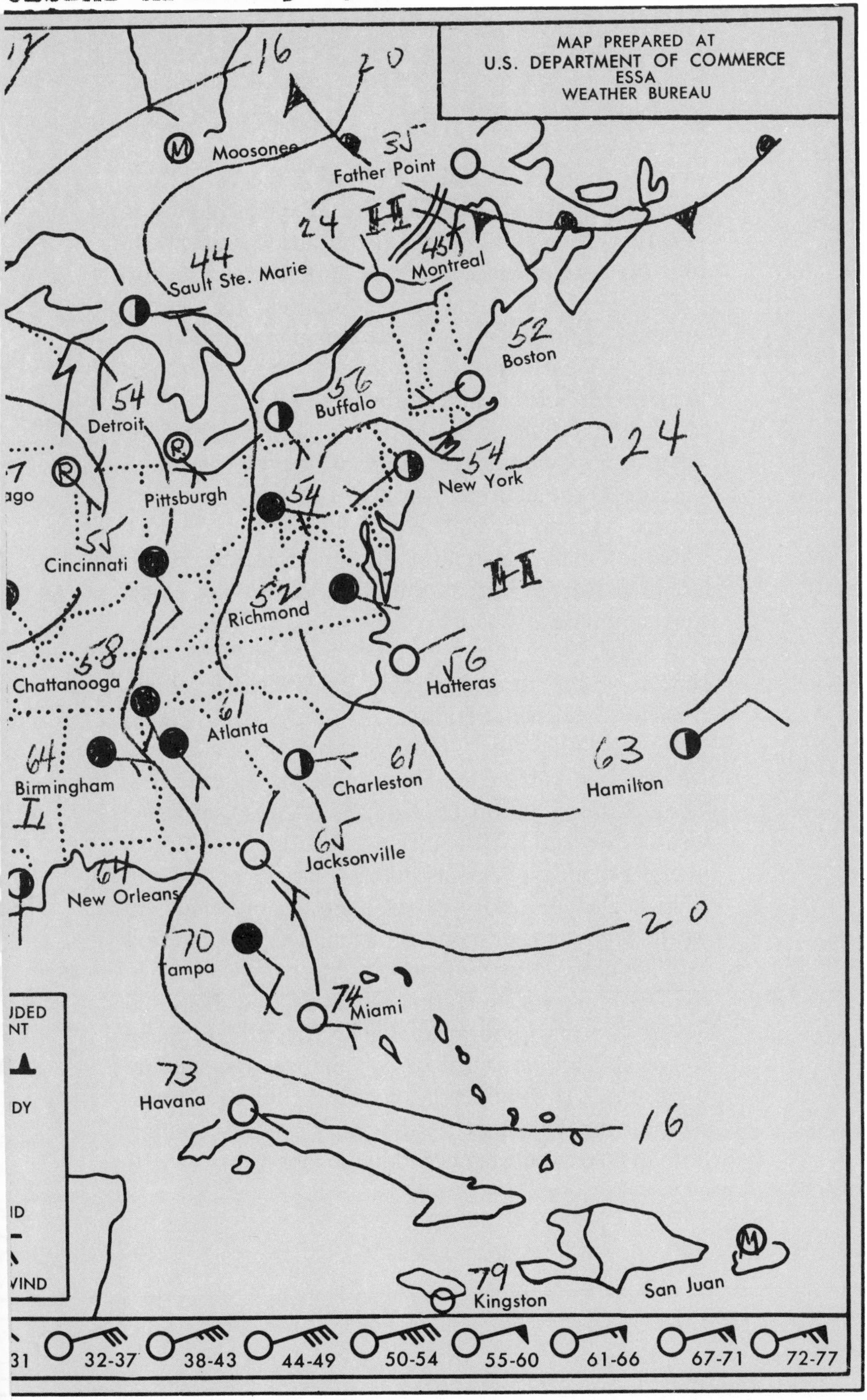

MAP PREPARED AT
U.S. DEPARTMENT OF COMMERCE
ESSA
WEATHER BUREAU

A-5452   USCOMM-ESSA-DC

weather forecast. It issues a "30-day forecast" which gives the weather outlook for the next month in general terms. The bureau also issues special warning forecasts of violent storms, hurricanes, and tornadoes. In winter and cooler months, the bureau issues warnings of possible freezing temperatures which are particularly valuable to the citrus fruit growers of Florida and California.

Weather stations along major rivers issue forecasts of flood conditions. A fire warning service aids in forest protection. Agricultural bulletins summarize regional weather conditions for farmers. Climatological information is also released by the Weather Bureau in the form of tables, graphs, maps, and summaries.

A special service supplies detailed, hourly weather reports, route forecasts, and local weather conditions for the benefit of pilots.

In July 1965, the United States Weather Bureau was made a part of the Environmental Science Services Administration (ESSA). ESSA also sponsors weather research through the Institute of Atmospheric Sciences. The institute's studies range from small-scale laboratory experiments to regional and world-wide surveys based on exchanges of data and satellite observations with other nations.

ESSA's research stations include the National Severe Storms Laboratory, the National Hurricane Research Laboratory, as well as the weather satellite programs. At Boulder, Colorado, ESSA's Atmospherics and Chemistry Laboratory studies weather both in field experiments and in the laboratory.

122

Government officials estimate that by increasing accurate weather forecasts to just five days ahead, savings in the United States alone might total $3 billion in agriculture, $100 million in transportation, $75 million in retailing, and $45 million in the lumber industry. Tomorrow's weather today is decidedly everybody's business.

12   In the Future

All nations share in the earth's atmosphere. Weather knows no national boundaries. The patterns of today's weather in Japan will reach the west coast of the United States in some form in three or four days. The weather patterns of the East Coast

will reach Europe in three or four days. A knowledge of all the world's weather is essential in making accurate long-range predictions.

The World Weather Watch holds out the promise of giving weathermen the information they need. By the 1970s, surface and upper-air observations from all participating nations will be pouring into three

World Weather Centers: Washington and Moscow in the Northern Hemisphere and Melbourne, Australia, in the Southern Hemisphere. High-speed communications circuits will link the world centers to each other and also to regional and national centers.

Satellites and other modern observing instruments will add to the immense amount of data pouring into the world centers. The centers will be outfitted with high-speed electronic computers and other equipment. They will collect, process, and send out global weather observations and forecasts to regional and national weather bureaus. The global forecasts will be used by the national bureaus to give more accurate forecasts for local regions.

The World Weather Watch will provide all nations with earlier, more accurate warnings of storms and other severe weather. It will make international travel by ship and plane safer and more efficient. It will allow better planning of agriculture, water management, fuel distribution, and transportation.

Watching the weather is not as dramatic as man's next step: changing the weather. Man has always changed weather to some extent. Even lighting a match warms a small bit of air and affects weather in a tiny way. Changing the weather on a larger scale has also been tried. Orange growers use smudge pots and blowers to protect their groves in cold temperatures. Gasoline is sometimes burned along airfield runways to get rid of fog.

Perhaps the beginning of modern weather-changing occurred on November 13, 1946. On that day, long trails of snow seemed to follow a small plane's path through a cloud. Inside the plane, Vincent Schaefer cranked out bits of dry ice into the cloud. The plane banked and made another run through the cloud. There was no doubt this time. By dropping dry ice, a very cold substance, into a certain kind of cloud, Schaefer had produced the first man-made snowstorm. It was a first step in man's attempt to control the weather.

Since that time, much work has been done with cloud-seeding experiments. Later experiments involved the use of silver-iodide smoke and other substances. Seeding has been used to clear fogs over airports and has opened huge holes in clouds. Research seems to show that seeding results in a 10 to 20 percent increase in precipitation over an area. But much work still remains to be done on this problem.

Even larger projects are being discussed by scientists. For example, it was suggested that carbon dust be used to blacken the ice fields of the Arctic. This would absorb more of the heat from sunlight and gradually warm the land beneath. In this way, the weather and climate of the entire Northern Hemisphere would be changed enough to make far northern lands livable. However, the amount of dust that would be needed seems too great to be practical.

Another idea was to explode a series of "clean" hydrogen bombs beneath the Arctic icecap. The steam produced by the immense heat would rise into the atmosphere, condense, and form clouds. The clouds would act as a blanket preventing the loss of heat into space and thus warming the atmosphere.

Still another idea was to dam the Bering Straits between Alaska and Siberia. Large, nuclear-powered pumps would be used to pour cold water from the Arctic Ocean into the Pacific Ocean. This would hopefully result in warm water from the Atlantic Ocean flowing into the Arctic and increasing its temperature.

There have been many other proposals, some on a smaller scale, some on a greater scale. But scientists need to learn much more before trying them out. Would they actually work? How much would they cost? What other regions would be affected and how? When we change the climate in one region, we may be changing the climate of the entire world. We have to learn much more before we attempt to do that.

But whatever the dangers, the goal of long-range weather control is something to work for. Man is beginning to accept the age-old challenge of doing something about the weather.

INDEX

Page numbers in **bold face** are illustrations.